Praise for *China in our Midst*

Filled with practical insights, tips and powerful changed-lives stories, *China In Our Midst* is a great read for the person wanting to engage the mission field of Chinese students and scholars scattered across America. Osborn and Su remind us how God moves people for His purposes. For years, the Lord has brought Chinese to our shores; students now but future leaders tomorrow! *China In Our Midst* challenges and equips us to embrace this supernatural opportunity to share the gospel with such a significant group of future global influencers.

TRAE VACEK
Executive Director, Bridges International
www.bridgesinternational.com

We are living in a historic moment. Chinese scholars are being welcomed into God's kingdom and he is using very normal Christians living near universities as his harvest laborers. The blend of stories from those coming to Christ, current research findings of recent converts, and practical lessons from a dynamic ministry working on over 50 campuses provides a rich tapestry of vision, challenge and guidance. Osborn and Su give us a clear picture of God's movement that is reshaping the leadership of China.

DR. ROY M. KING
Professor Emeritus, Columbia International University
Team Leader/Pastor, Market Common Church, Myrtle Beach, SC
www.royking.org

Four hundred thousand next-generation leaders of the biggest nation on earth: These are the Chinese students in American universities. When Jesus said, "Make disciples of all nations," he had them in his heart. This book shares wisdom for discipling such students. Based on surveys, interviews, case studies, and thousands of hours of ministry experience, it tackles a range of issues—from the intriguing history of Christian witness in China, to the special challenge of witness to scholars who wrestle with deep spiritual questions in spite of scientific skepticism, to cross-cultural misunderstandings, and how to minimize them. There are 400,000 reasons why you should read this book.

MIRIAM ADENEY, PH.D.
Associate Professor of Global and Urban Ministries, Seattle Pacific University
Author, *Kingdom Without Borders: The Untold Story of Global Christianity*

This thought-provoking, informative treatise, based on the doctoral research of Dr. Osborn and the ministry of Rev. Su, is compelling—China could have more Christians than any other country by 2030! Osborn and Su write with passion, illustrating with powerful statistics and heart-warming stories the factors which encourage Chinese to come to Christ and those which impede their doing so. Everyone in international relations and every church and individual seeking to share the love of Jesus should read this book! The power of Christ in millions of lives will be a blessing to this great nation!

DR. LOIS A. DODDS
Co-founder/President, Heartstream Resources for Cross-cultural Workers, Inc.

Osborn and Su bring a unique combination of leadership, experience, and understanding of Chinese culture to bear on a critical issue: reaching Chinese intellectuals with the message of Christ. Understanding that "this is a key moment in time to impact the largest country in the world," the authors lay out key principles and practical ideas for effective ministry. Those engaged in—or desiring to learn more about—outreach among Chinese students and scholars in America should read this insightful work.

REV. BEAU MILLER
Executive Director, Association of Christians Ministering Among Internationals (ACMI) www.acmi-ism.org

The unique contribution of the blended bi-cultural perspectives and practical recommendations of co-authors Osborn and Su, along with relevant research findings, distinguish *China in Our Midst* as an outstanding resource for volunteers and ministers engaged in service among Chinese students in North America. But equally valuable are the extensive quotes of Chinese scholars who believed and received the gospel in America, that render this book a powerful and appropriate gift for Chinese seekers.

LEITON E. CHINN
Lausanne Catalyst for International Student Ministries

This book surely has put a smile on God's face. Why? For at least two reasons: first, because there is now in print a tool which matches the need of equipping the American church to effectively befriend Chinese students among us; and second, because it offers the means by which local churches and regular Christians can have a global impact. Want to know how you can transform China for eternity? Get this book, read it, practice it, and then, enjoy the journey!

DR. CHRISTOPHER R. LITTLE
Missiologist-at-Large

For more than five decades, China Outreach Ministries has been on the forefront of reaching Chinese students and scholars with the Gospel. In *China in our Midst*, Daniel Su and Glen Osborn draw upon their own rich experience, as well as that of their COM colleagues and others, to present a multi-faceted portrait of what is arguably one of the most strategic ministry opportunities in the world today. Packed with historical context and valuable cross-cultural insights backed up by current survey research, this book will serve as an indispensable guide to those engaged in Chinese student outreach.

DR. BRENT FULTON
President, ChinaSource
www.chinasource.org

China in Our Midst is a very rich read. I highly recommend it for anyone who cares about China and American-Chinese relations. It is a "must" as a handbook for those in ministry to Chinese, but has much wisdom for outreach to other internationals and cross-cultural ministry as a whole. I have known COM's work for several decades and have been impressed by its thoughtful, strategic approach to ministry, its care for staff and volunteers including empowering mainland Chinese workers, and its integrity and Godly approach to succession under three able leaders in turn. This book is the latest example of its initiative and leadership in partnering with others for the Kingdom.

DR. CAROL LEE HAMRIN
China specialist, Global China Center
Author, *China and the Challenge of the Future*

American churches have often overlooked the most promising and important mission field in the world that is sitting on their doorstep: the 400,000 Chinese students and scholars who are attending university in the US. Glen Osborn and Daniel Su's important book, *China in our Midst*, shows beyond any doubt how important this mission field is and how American Christians can be deployed in it with real effectiveness.

DR. DAVID AIKMAN
Former Beijing Bureau Chief for *Time* magazine
Author, *Jesus in Beijing*

Glen and Daniel present clear, practical, and compelling reasons for Christians to engage with the Chinese internationals God is sending to the USA. Their insights combined with solid research and personal stories make this a must read for all who want to understand and serve Chinese internationals.

RICHARD MENDOLA
Executive Director, International Friendships, Inc.

China in our Midst

China in our Midst

Reaching Chinese International
Students in America

Glen Osborn & Daniel B. Su

China Outreach Ministries

Mechanicsburg, Pennsylvania

China in our Midst: Reaching Chinese International Students in America

By Glen Osborn and Daniel B. Su
Copyright © 2016 by Chinese Outreach Ministries

555 Gettysburg Rd
Mechanicsburg, PA 17055
www.chinaoutreach.org

China Outreach Ministries shares Christ's love with Chinese students and scholars from North American campuses, serving them, reaching them with the Good News, discipling them, and helping them become godly leaders for Christ who share their faith with others.

Cover and interior book design by Kelly Smith, Tallgrass Media.
Cover image from pixabay.com, Creative Commons licensed (CC0).

10 9 8 7 6 5 4 3 2 1

ISBN-13: 978-0-692-85736-6

Dedicated to the memory of Rev. Earnest Hummer,
President of China Outreach Ministries 1982-2001,
our mentor and friend.

Contents

Acknowledgments

We would like to thank our families and friends for their patience and encouragement in this process. We also want to thank the COM board, leadership and staff for providing support, information and connections. We appreciate our wives, Beth Su and Betty Osborn, for their support and contributions to this book. Most importantly, we thank our Heavenly Father, for his love and leadership in our lives. He is the One who has opened this amazing door of opportunity.

Introduction

The opportunity to share the gospel with the top thinkers of China is a vital and growing harvest field. At this writing, approximately 400,000 Chinese are students and scholars at American universities. This is the largest group of international students in America. Chinese students currently account for 29% of all foreign students studying in the United States (Newman 2014).

We (Glen and Daniel) have the opportunity to be a part of Christian outreach to this key group of people through China Outreach Ministries (COM). It is a faith based ministry focused on giving Christ to China's future leaders through developing relationships with Chinese on university campuses and sharing with them the love and truth of Jesus Christ.

Today COM has personnel strategically placed at over fifty universities in the United States. Our driving passion is for each Chinese scholar who comes to America to have the opportunity to hear the gospel and respond, but the numbers of Chinese at universities in the United States are much greater than any one ministry can impact alone. This is a significant moment in history with great potential impact on the future of China and the world. At the same time, there are many Christians in key locations in the United States who could impact the people of a country on the other side of the globe by simply opening the door of their home and inviting in a stranger. The church in North America must be informed and encouraged to act in this God-ordained moment of history. We have seen that when Christians reach out in love and the light of Christ is seen in their lives, many Chinese students and scholars respond to Jesus.

Therefore, this book is written to inform and inspire those currently involved in Chinese student ministry, as well as those who could and will be involved. Our desire is that all Chinese who come to study in the United States would have the opportunity to understand and experience the truth and love of Jesus Christ, and that many would return home to China transformed by him. For this to become a reality, more Christians in North America must be passionately involved.

In December of 2014, I (Glen) finished a Doctor in Ministry in Missions at Columbia International University. My dissertation focused on factors encouraging or impeding the process of making disciples among Chinese scholars in the United States. Over sixty Chinese scholars who have become Christians since coming to study in America were interviewed and their answers compiled and studied. This study again affirmed the open opportunity before us, and how God is demonstrating his love in reaching the Chinese with the gospel. We will be sharing the findings of this study in this book.

We are writing this book together to give the reader a perspective that includes the writing of a Caucasian American and a Mainland Chinese. Our hope is that you will be able to gain insight not only through the factors discovered in the research, but also through the cultural understandings that will be shared. Glen served as President of China Outreach Ministries from 2001 to 2016 and now serves as Minister at Large with COM. Daniel joined the organization in 1991 as a campus minister and began three new campus ministries. He left for seven years to plant a church in Katy, Texas, and returned in 2014 to serve as Executive Vice President. He became the President of COM in 2017.

In writing this book, for the sake of security and privacy, we have intentionally altered the names of individuals in their personal stories, but their stories and experiences remain true and valuable.

We will be addressing some aspects of differences between Chinese and American cultures. We want to share what we have learned — from our experiences and even from our mistakes — in order to help our readers. However, we are keenly aware that there is an inherent limitation in describing cultural differences in general terms because it runs the risk of sounding stereotypical and failing to view individuals as individuals.

On the other hand, we want to recognize that to a certain degree we are all products of our own culture, and as such we are not totally immune to the influences of our cultural environments, no matter how hard we may try. So, in dealing with cultural differences, it is imperative that we strive to be truthful, even if that means occasionally sounding politically incorrect. And, of course, we want to always consciously uphold our value that all human beings are created, valued and loved by God. Likewise, we Christians want to value and love all human beings and treat them with respect and dignity regardless of their cultural practices, with which we may or may not agree.

We live in a multi-cultural society, and it is important to not naively equate what is ethnic to what is cultural. An ethnically Chinese person who lived most of his life in the US is more American culturally than a Caucasian American who lived most of his life in Africa.

When Gary Locke, a Chinese American, was appointed by President Obama as the US ambassador to China in 2011, many Chinese naively regarded him as one of their own, without realizing that Ambassador Locke was American and acted with the best interests of the United States in his mind.

We want to clearly state our position that, while cultural differences do exist, each human being remains a unique individual and deserves to be viewed and treated as such. There is no place for stereotyping in Christian ministry. In the same manner, we also want to guard against the temptation of trying to explain every difference as cultural. The reality is, when a difference emerges between a Chinese and an American, it may not always be a cultural difference; it might very well be a personal difference. Unfortunately, in our society today, people tend to assume that any variance between two people of different cultural or ethnic backgrounds must be cultural, and then act accordingly. They thus fail to recognize the difference could very well be a personal one.

In this book we will be addressing cultural differences, but we want to keep in mind that as human beings created in God's image and affected by the fall of Adam and Eve, we also share a lot in common. We all long for meaning and purpose in life; we all desire to be respected and loved; we all wish the best for our children and our nation; we all desire to see a world free of suffering and injustices; we all deal with temptations and the dark side of our human nature; and we all hope the future will be better for our children.

Part 1

Background and Context

Chapter 1

The Open Door of Opportunity

In 1978, Deng Xaioping decided to send 3,000 scholars overseas in order to rebuild China's academic community, which had been devastated by the anti-intellectual Cultural Revolution. It was a key historical moment for such a large country to entrust the future of its top thinkers to education in other nations. The relatively small group of scholars that came in 1978 had grown to over 300,000 by 2015. And today this includes not only visiting scholars, but also various levels of graduate students, Ph.D. students, undergraduates, visiting scholars, and accompanying family members. In addition, there is a growing number of Chinese high school students sent by their parents so that they may seamlessly move into American college opportunities. In order for these students and scholars to study in the United States, they must qualify scholastically, have the financial resources to attend either through scholarships or family support, and have the determination to make it through the academic challenges as a second culture student. There is great opportunity, for as China continues to move forward as a significant world power, many of the people who will make the decisions for China's future are currently in the United States.

Lee Kuan Yew, former Prime Minister of Singapore and China

observer stated, "America's greatest long term influence on China comes from playing host to the thousands of students who come from China each year, some of the ablest Chinese scholars and scientists. They will be the most powerful agents for change in China." [1]

This opportunity has eternal significance as top thinkers from China are in North America and are open to hear the gospel. Many of these intellectuals are returning to key positions in China after studying overseas. "More than 350,000 Chinese returned from overseas study in 2013, up from just 20,000 ten years earlier. They accounted for almost one-quarter of the 1.4 million who had returned in total since 1978. So great are the numbers that there is a derogatory term for those who are unable to find work: *hai dai,* which means seaweed but also sounds like "[returning from] abroad and waiting." [2]

There are many reasons for the growing number of returnees, but it seems due mainly to the growing economy in China and greater opportunities there. Those who have become committed followers of Jesus return to China and demonstrate the fruit of the Spirit to those around them.

Yang is an example of the impact of one who returns to China as a follower of Jesus. He came to America for his graduate studies and was befriended by Christians, who cared for him and shared the gospel. He eventually came to believe, and grew in his faith. Yang married, got a good job, and moved up in company leadership. He also was deeply involved in a local church and eventually served as the head elder. The Spirit of God challenged him to return to China with his family, and after much time praying and then preparing, they

---

1   Allison 2013, under "Can US policies and actions significantly influence China's trajectory and behavior as it emerges as a great power?"

2   http://monitor.icef.com/2015/05/chinese-enrolment-in-the-us-shifting-increasingly-to-undergraduate-studies/

did return. Since returning, he has shared his faith with his family and seen many respond to Christ. When he returned to China, he worked in upper leadership and was the only Christian in the office. After one year there were twelve others. Today he owns his own company, and has been the key person in developing several churches in his city.

Samuel Ling, director of China Horizon, asks a challenging question: "If China does become a world leader, will Christian ideas influence her direction? Her goals?" He discusses the importance of learning from history, pointing out that in the early 1900s when Communist students led an anti-Christian movement, Western Christians were not prepared to respond. Today, there is an opportunity to interact with Chinese intellectuals who are searching for a worldview for the future of China. This is another chance to share Jesus Christ and answer their questions. "What does Jesus have to say to China's political, economic, cultural, educational, and family needs? Will Christianity offer a viable voice to shape China's future?" (Ling 1999, 6-7).

This is a key moment in time to connect with people from the largest country in the world and a country that continues to grow in world influence. This opportunity is happening through contacts with top Chinese intellectuals at universities in North America. God has provided an open door to Christians in North America to share the love and truth of Jesus Christ with the "foreigner" or "alien" from Mainland China.

God's Heart for the Foreigner

Throughout the Scriptures, we see God's heart expressed for his people to care for the foreigner or alien. He speaks to Israel to show love and care to them as one of their own (Lev. 19:33-34; Exod. 23:9; Deut. 10:19). Solomon prays for God's blessing on the foreigner so that all the nations would know him (2 Chr. 6:33). And the Psalmist speaks of the Lord watching over the foreigner (Ps. 146:9).

In the New Testament, Jesus includes inviting in strangers in his list of ways that his people minister to him (Matt. 25:35). Throughout Acts, the Spirit of God leads the apostles to reach out beyond their own people. We see God leading Philip to the Ethiopian official, who had come to Israel seeking God (Acts 8:26-40). This person of influence from a completely different cultural background went back home to leadership in his country knowing and rejoicing in the Lord.

God moves people for his purposes, in order that the gospel may reach all people. He is moving thousands from China to come to the United States for education and study. He is moving many Christians in the United States to reach out in love. The problem is that the number of those reaching out is far from meeting the need and responding to the opportunity. A generous estimate would be that only 10-15% of Chinese students and scholars who come to America have the opportunity to hear of the love of God for them through a caring Christian. This is a white harvest field, and Jesus speaks with regard to a vast opportunity: "The harvest is plentiful but the workers are few. Ask the Lord of the harvest, therefore, to send out workers into his harvest field" (Matt. 9:37-38). We are to pray to the Lord of the harvest for laborers for this white harvest field. God's solution to meeting the need is to pray for people to be led by his Spirit to answer the call and respond to the need.

There are certainly adequate numbers of Christians to reach out to all of these Chinese students and scholars. Many churches and ministries, however, do not see reaching out to international students as a viable Christian missionary outreach. We need to help spread the news that this is a viable, effective way that God is providing to reach the nation of China with the gospel. It is also more economical, and it is an open door to meet with top academics that have almost non-existent exposure to the gospel in their own country.

Chapter 2

Standing on the Shoulders of Giants

The current opportunities to share the gospel with Chinese intellectuals are amazing and the opportunities exceed expectations as well as laborers. But this is a relatively recent phenomenon. We stand upon the shoulders of giants who in days past have given their lives, and fortunes, to boldly take the gospel to the people of China. The history of China Outreach Ministries is connected to this time in the history of missions to China.

Hudson Taylor

Hudson Taylor is a name closely associated with taking Christ to the Chinese. China Inland Mission, now OMF International, came into being as a result of Taylor's obedience to God's call, giving his life for the sake of Chinese knowing Christ. One of his famous sayings clearly demonstrates this calling. "If I had a thousand pounds China should have it—if I had a thousand lives, China should have them. No! Not China, but Christ. Can we do too much for him? Can we do enough for such a precious Saviour?"

Before Hudson Taylor was born, his parents had prayed that their child would be a missionary to China. Early in life he personally had the desire to follow that prayer, but in his teen years began to drift away from the things of God. But after a conversion experience, he began to actively serve the Lord, and in 1853 he left England by boat for China with the Chinese Evangelistic Society. He arrived in Shanghai in March of 1854. Having a different perspective on funding ministry, he resigned from the Chinese Evangelistic Society in 1857. After experiencing much tragedy, including the death of his wife, he returned to England but he was still passionate about reaching the Chinese for Christ.

The following is from the OMF International website:

"Hudson Taylor wanted to reach the Chinese in the rural and inland areas. He was convinced a new mission was needed for the task. However, the idea of shouldering such a burden troubled him. Suddenly, while on Brighton Beach a fresh truth dawned; the responsibility was not his but God's! On the flyleaf of his Bible he wrote, "Prayed for the 24 willing, skillful laborers at Brighton, June 25, 1865."

Hudson Taylor knew that there were millions of people who needed to hear the message of Jesus Christ and thus named the mission's magazine *China's Millions*. It is still published today as *East Asia's Millions.*

Together with his co-workers, Hudson Taylor began speaking and preaching and distributing literature. However, when he saw that the Chinese people could only see him as an outsider, he followed the example of Dr. Charles Gutzlaff, whom he called the "grandfather of the China Inland Mission," and chose to wear the clothes of the common Chinese people. Although this made him the laughing stock of both foreign and Chinese onlookers, the effects proved his point and helped people see that what he preached was not such a foreign message after all.

While stressing the need to preach widely, Hudson Taylor also emphasized that local churches needed to be established and matured, that church buildings be of Chinese and not foreign design, and that leaders of the churches should be Chinese Christians. His burden for the still unreached areas pressed him further. The first party of 18 sailed for China in 1866, and 18 more in 1870. In 1886, he issued another call for 100 new workers in two years, and 102 were sent by the end of 1887. In 1888, the first North American party was sent out.

Lottie Moon

Many have heard of Lottie Moon because of the annual Christmas offering taken in the Southern Baptist churches for missions. This offering began in 1888 when Lottie Moon was a Southern Baptist missionary in China and appealed to the church for more missionaries and funds to meet the need and opportunity in China. The first offering raised $3,315, enough to send three additional missionaries. Since its beginning, the Lottie Moon offering has resulted in over $1.5 billion for overseas missions. Lottie Moon served in China for 40 years, arriving in 1873, joining her sister Edmonia. She first served as a teacher at a boy's school, but discovered that her passion was evangelism—sharing Christ with those who had not heard of his amazing love and grace. She was in China during very trying times, facing political unrest, war, and famine. In 1912, at age 72, she died on the way back to the United States for medical care. She was only 50 pounds, due to sharing her resources with others during a devastating famine. She gave her life for the salvation of the Chinese.

The Cambridge Seven

The Cambridge Seven were six students from Cambridge

University and one from the Royal Military Academy who left their promising futures in England to become missionaries to China in 1885. Before leaving for China to serve with China Inland Mission, the seven toured Universities in England and Scotland, challenging students to give their lives to take the gospel to China. Their testimonies impacted many, also contributing to the development of the Student Volunteer Movement in America.

The Pyke Family

China Outreach Ministries' roots go back to a contemporary of Hudson Taylor, Lottie Moon and the Cambridge Seven. In 1873, James Howell Pyke I and his brand new bride Annabel, left Indiana on their wedding day, traveling to the west coast of America to take a ship to China as missionaries. The trip to China took 65 days in a paddle wheeler, similar those that traveled the Mississippi River. They landed in the northern port city of Tientsin in mid-winter, to give their lives to a land and people they had never known for the sake of the gospel. The Pykes had eight children. One of their sons, Reverend Frederick Merrill Pyke (1884-1976), was also a missionary in North China. Frederick married Frances Louise Taft, also born of missionaries in China (the Reverend and Mrs. Marcus L. Taft). During World War II, Frances and Frederick were interned by the Japanese military for 30 months in the prison camp at Weihsien, China. They had three children: Louise, Ruth, and James. James Howell Pyke's grandson and namesake, James Pyke also served in China as a missionary. The Pyke family served in China as missionaries for three generations.

Due to the takeover of China by the Communists, missionaries were forced to leave. The Pykes left in 1949 to return to the United States. On their return, they had contact in London with a Chinese pastor friend there—Stephen Wang—who was reaching out with the gospel to Chinese students. He had formed a ministry called Chinese Overseas Christian Mission or COCM. The Pykes decided to help with this ministry and begin a partner organization in the United States to raise funds for the ministry, as well as to develop other outreach to Chinese. In 1959, Chinese Overseas Christian Mission was chartered in the United States.

As was true in the case of Hudson Taylor, much of the ministry in China in the late 19th and early 20th centuries was focused on peasants and farmers in rural areas. There were very few inroads with intellectuals, leaders, and other top professionals. It was not that missionaries did not desire to have these opportunities, but rather the open doors among the millions in China were to the poor and downtrodden. Also, the powerful and successful were not interested in the "superstitious" pursuits that attracted the less educated. But the prayers and sacrifices of those who have gone before have been honored by God and today doors have been opened to share Christ's truth and love with the top thinkers of China. We truly do stand on the shoulders of giants.

Chapter 3

A Brief Overview of Chinese Intellectuals Encountering Christianity

The Nestorians

The Nestorians were the earliest Christians who went to the Chinese capital Chang-An (or Xian-An today) around 635 during the reign of Emperor Tai Zong of the Tang Dynasty. The Chinese were known for their hospitality and the emperor granted a lot of freedom to the missionaries, who reached out to China's elite ruling class and presented Christian teachings by using Chinese terms and concepts familiar to the Chinese. This is evidenced by the historical artifacts still in display in China (see figures 1 and 2).

The Jesuits

Jesuit missionaries came to China by focusing their efforts on the ruling elites in the sixteenth century. They succeeded in introducing Christian faith to the Chinese in a culturally appropriate manner. The Jesuits won the following of top Ming Dynasty imperial court officials

Figure 1. The Nestorian Stele in Xi-An, China, 781 AD.

Figure 2. Restoration of a Nestorian image of Jesus Christ during China's Tang Dynasty dating back to the 9th century.

such as Xu Guangqi (1562-1633), Yang Tingyun (1562-1627), and Li Zhizao (1565-1630). Even Kangxi, the Chinese Emperor then, professed faith in Christ and was said to be ready for baptism.

Overall, the Jesuits made conscious efforts in differentiating what was fundamentally Christian from what was culturally European. They also tried to not unnecessarily demand changes in Chinese cultural expressions.

Matteo Ricci (1552-1610) is perhaps the best-known Jesuit missionary. He and his fellow missionaries won the favor of the Chinese Emperor, who gave them one of the best pieces of land in the heart of Beijing for their missionary compound. Ironically, the compound now houses the Beijing Communist Party school for training government officials for the City of Beijing. The Chinese government honors Ricci by keeping his tomb by the gate of the school, so in a sense his witness continues even today.

Despite their success, the Jesuits' cultural sensitivity to the Chinese was challenged by the conservative wing of the Catholic Church in what was known as the Rites Controversy. A key issue had to do with the way the Chinese traditionally honored their deceased ancestors by burning incense and paper money. The Jesuits interpreted it as a Chinese way of "honoring" the ancestors and therefore a cultural expression while the conservatives interpreted it as "a worship" and therefore a religious expression. The Pope sided with the conservatives by banning Chinese believers from such traditional practices.

The Pope's decision angered the Chinese Emperor. In an act of retaliation, the Emperor issued an edict to the missionaries, criticizing them for their ignorance of Chinese culture and lack of cultural sensitivities. Soon after that, the missionaries were told to leave China.

Tragically, contact between the East and the West was cut off for many centuries. It wasn't until after British gunboats forced China open following the Opium War in the early nineteenth century that Protestant missionaries had another opportunity to enter China.

Through the lens of hindsight, some scholars view this unfortunate series of events as one of the great might-have-beens in church history, and even in world history. It could have been the "Constantine moment" for China if the church had been more understanding of the Chinese ways of doing things, or if the Pope had sided with the more open-minded contingent of the missionaries. Some scholars have pointed out that if China had embraced the Christian faith in the seventeenth century, global history would have taken a radically different path and we would be living in a much different world today.

Protestant Missionary Movements

China was forced to its knees by the British after a humiliating defeat in the Opium War (1839–1842). Protestant missionaries seized the open-door opportunities and entered China. Pioneered by Robert Morrison (1782-1834), missionaries from various protestant denominations went to China and engaged in a wide range of activities ranging from education, medicine, cultural exchanges, social work, to preaching and church planting. The number of Chinese converts grew rapidly from about 100,000 baptized believers in 1900 to about 330,000 baptized believers and 270,000 communicants.

The missionaries came from a wide variety of backgrounds. Some were top intellectuals, graduates of elite universities in the West, and others were ordinary lay believers who felt called by God to serve the Chinese. Some of China's top universities today were established by missionaries, including Beijing University, originally called Yanjing University.

Missionaries had some success in reaching out to China's intellectuals. According to Daniel H. Bays in his book *A New History of Christianity in China*, some Chinese converts went overseas for study and later returned to serve in China:

> Some of these intellectuals joined the faculty of Yanjing University (the predecessor of world renowned Peking University or Beijing University), including Liu Tingfang (a prolific scholar, returned from his Ph.D. in the US), Zhao Zichen (perhaps modern China's foremost Christian theologian who had studied in America from 1914 to 1917), Hong Ye (William Hung, a scholar with deep

intellectual roots both in the West and Chinese tradition), and Wu Leichuan who came to Christianity in mid-life and became the first Chinese chancellor of Yanjing University for eight years.

The Protestant missionary movement had left a lasting impact on China even after missionaries were forced out of China after the communist takeover of the country in 1949. The church in China has not only survived under the communist rule but also grown to be a powerful witness in society today.

Although missionaries went to China for religious reasons, the timing was unfortunate because the Chinese saw them as following the Western gunboats and military forces. Some Chinese even viewed Christianity as a Western cultural invasion of China after its military invasion. This ill timing was to haunt Christian ministry for many years to come and contributed to the May Fourth Movement in China, which was triggered by China's humiliation at the Versailles during the Peace Conference of 1919. The Movement, led by the leading Chinese intellectuals, was anti-West. Among the unfortunate easy targets were Christian missionaries and even Chinese Christians.

The Contemporary Outreach to Intellectuals

In the decades since China adopted its Open Door policy to the outside world under the leadership of Deng Xiao Ping, Christians have been engaged in a wide variety of ministry activities in reaching out to Chinese intellectuals both in China and outside of China. Opportunities continue to abound. Many Christians take teaching positions in China and bear Christian witness through their professions. Numerous others have gone into China through business or cultural exchange channels.

At the same time, many Chinese have come to America and other countries for study and research. This opens up opportunities for Christians to serve the Chinese and at the same time to share their faith. For example, in the United States alone, it is estimated that there are over 300,000 Chinese students and scholars on US university campuses plus their family members. Many of these students have come to embrace Christian faith through the outreach efforts of Christian groups or individuals.

Many China experts have noted that China's cream of the crop is here in the West, particularly in the United States. Many of Beijing's top leaders send their children to study here. Speaking at a fundraising event for China Outreach Ministries, David Aikman commented on the disproportional large influential role China's intellectuals have had throughout history. Pointing to the presence of hundreds of Chinese students and scholars in the US, he concluded: "Reaching out to students from the People's Republic of China is simply the most strategically important Christian missionary endeavor in the world."

God has given us an opportunity to build on the legacy of the Nestorians, the Jesuits, and other early missionaries to make an impact on China's future leaders, many of whom are right here at our doorstep.

Chapter 4

You Can Make a Difference

While opportunities were limited for early missionaries to reach out to Chinese intellectuals, that is not the case today. With over 300,000 Chinese students and scholars at universities in the United States, the opportunity to develop friendly relationships is clearly before our eyes. The future leaders of China are in America today. Brent Fulton of China Source has shared that a growing portion of the members of the Communist Politburo and Central Committee have studied overseas, and there will come a time when all of those in leadership will have at one time been overseas as students and researchers. The current President of China, Xi Jinping, came to the United States in 1985 to do agricultural research in Iowa. While in the United States, he stayed in an American family's home. When he returned as the Chinese Vice President in 2012, he insisted on visiting this place again since it had been such a special time in his life.

Our research has shown that love and friendship with Christ followers in the United States is God's method for thousands of Chinese students and scholars to not only be exposed to Christian love and truth, but also to come to personal faith in Jesus Christ. When Christians are intentional in befriending a Chinese student or scholar, God uses that connection for his eternal purposes. We encourage training and preparation, but those are not really the key elements. It is life-on-life interaction that makes the greatest difference. It is simply being willing to open one's life to the Chinese among us.

Take for example Bruce. Bruce was an elderly man in Boston. Bruce loved Jesus and desired to serve him faithfully to the end of his life on earth. Bruce placed an advertisement on the message board at Harvard University asking for someone to help him learn Mandarin. He asked for someone who was a Christian and Chinese. Earlier that year, Liu had come to Harvard to study law in the Graduate School. Liu had been a member of the police in China and had been involved in raiding secret places of worship and arresting those in attendance. In 1989, when the Chinese government took drastic action against student protestors at Tiananmen Square, killing many and arresting others, Liu was very troubled and disoriented. In his time of inner struggle, a friend encouraged him to go to America and continue his studies. He was able to get accepted to Harvard, and lived in an apartment complex that housed mainly divinity school students. He was intrigued by the courses that these divinity students were taking, and began to audit classes. Liu liked what he heard and read about Jesus—the philosophy that he understood Jesus to be teaching, and the way of life that Jesus lived. He began to consider himself a Christian, so when he saw Bruce's advertisement, he responded. Liu met with Bruce regularly at Bruce's home. He asked Bruce why he wanted to learn Mandarin, and Bruce replied, "I don't have many years left to live, so I want to make the most of the time and have the greatest impact for Jesus that I can. The Chinese are the largest group of people in the world, so if I can learn Mandarin, I can communicate with them and share Jesus with them." Bruce was not good at learning Mandarin, but Liu really enjoyed his time with him. He enjoyed the fatherly love that Bruce shared with him, and he was attracted to something in his life that was hard to explain.

One day Liu received communication that his father was very ill and was not expected to live. Liu immediately returned to China but did not reach there in time to see his father alive. He was emotionally crushed by this loss, but even more so when he returned to Boston and found that Bruce had died. In his time of grief, Liu continued to be touched by Bruce's life and testimony for Jesus. Liu cried out to Jesus and he found the life he had seen in Bruce. Today, Liu is a pastor who has planted churches that are reaching Chinese in the US and has been involved in equipping pastors in China. This man who persecuted pastors is now training them. God used an older man named Bruce. And God can use you.

Part Two

General Principles of Ministry Among the Chinese

Chapter 5

Understanding the Mainland Scholar

The Needs of the Chinese Scholar in America

Fenggang Yang says that "a deep sense of homelessness" is a factor in Chinese scholars being receptive. He also states that because of extreme changes in China, they are "without cultural traditions as barriers" and "are now both free and bound to seek alternate meaning systems" (1998, 250-1). Christianity is attractive due to the fact that they find absolutes and certainty in their disrupted and changing world experience. One Chinese scholar stated: "During my years at Dartmouth, I have often been paralyzed by the two fundamental questions posed by immortality. What is my life for? Why am I here? Having no answer upsets me. The cultural displacement undercut my self-confidence" (Garrod 1999, 163).

In her Th.D. dissertation at Boston University School of Theology, Lai Fan Wong shares that leaving a familiar environment and culture is an uprooting shock, and coming to a new country results in great stress. She cites research showing that this situation results in experiences of separation, loss, homesickness, and loneliness (2006, 19). She goes on to state that "it is important for the new arrivals to find a new network with which to mingle in order to understand the new environment and balance their previous loss" (2006, 20). McKnight states "if a country or region is going through a crisis cycle, more conversions occur; if a society is highly stable and happy, fewer conversions occur" (2002, 61).

Chinese scholars are at American universities because they are top performers and highly driven people. They are under pressure to perform and live with high expectations from family and country. In this stress and struggle, there is openness to the gospel. In a study of Chinese scholars at two mid-western universities, Wang notes that, "a common theme running through almost all of the conversion stories was strong dissatisfaction with the materialism or money-seeking milieu prevailing in China today" (2006, 185). He also mentions that the scholars see that what they have been taught about Christians in China is not true as they experience Christian ministers and believers as "normal people" and "that Christianity provides moral values in American society and that Christianity is a normal choice for college-educated people" (2006, 185). He suggests that testimonies by successful professionals in science and engineering are effective ways to impact Chinese scholars (2006, 186).

Chinese scholars in North America are under a high degree of pressure to adjust to a new culture, attempting to achieve in academics with limited language abilities and they also feel alone. They feel "helpless, powerless and meaningless" and as a result, "many have become religious seekers" (Yang 1999, 86).

In her qualitative research on Chinese Christians in North America, M.R. Daban repeatedly found that Chinese intellectuals who convert to Christianity are seeking "the survival of humanity," which includes finding the right values to promote human existence (2004, 20). This idealism among Chinese intellectuals who sojourn to North

America was mirrored by those who came here in the early 20th century (Bieler 2004, 5).

Cultural Perspectives of Chinese Scholars

Curiosity and desire to relate to a new culture provide opportunities for friendship and love in the name of Christ. Chinese scholars often have a perspective of Christianity being a part of American culture. They desire to have exposure to all aspects of this new culture.

> Yi-Qiang Xiong came to the United States for Ph.D. studies in grain science. He is a non-Christian but attends a Bible study organized by his American friends together with other students from China.... Xiong says he attends the Bible study unless he is too busy. His aim is "to learn something of the customs and religion of Americans." When asked if he is a Christian, Xiong laughs. It isn't a derisive laugh. It is gentle and apologetic. "No," he replies. "Not yet"... Xiong's wish to learn something of the customs and religion of Americans is honored. It provides an excellent opportunity for the Christian to study the Word of God with him. (Lau 1984, 83)

Chinese culture is collective in contrast to Western individualism. Wu shares that a Chinese person's identity is strongly tied to how others regard him or her. "Chinese can hardly conceive of themselves, not to mention God, apart from their web of relationships, since their identity and all that is significant is relational" (Wu 2013, 145). Social networks are an important consideration in effectively reaching Chinese intellectuals.

Rawson quotes Chinese anthropologist Longji Sun:

> In Chinese culture a man is defined in terms of a bilateral

relationship. This relationship is a matter of Sodality.... We may say that from birth a Chinese person is enclosed by a network of interpersonal relationships, which defines and organizes his existence, which controls his Heart-and-Mind. When a Chinese individual is not under the control of the Heart-and-Mind of others, he will become the most selfish of men and bring chaos both to himself and to those around him. And yet when the definition of his Sodality is extended to the entire community, he is capable of being the most unselfish of men. (Ling 1999, 159)

It is important to understand the relationship of scholars with others they are relating to while in America, but also their relationships with parents, family, friends, government and employment connections in China. There is a concern as to how their decisions will influence their relationships at home (Ling 1999, 161). When ministering to Chinese, identification of influential leaders and focused attention on them can significantly increase impact with all Chinese scholars.

Confucian principles are a guiding element in Chinese cultural perspectives. Yang states, "the attraction of evangelical Christianity to Chinese immigrants...comes from its perceived compatibility with Confucian moral values" (Yang 1998, 252).

It gives standards to a relative, confusing post-modern world and Chinese converts are pleased to apply these systematic values in their own lives and pass them on to the next generation in order to fight against the unhealthy development of "materialism, consumerism and eroticism" in the postmodern world. (Wong 2006, 46)

Confucian values include care for one's family and friends, thrift, education and humaneness. Scholars from China, looking for a belief system that works, are often open to Christian teaching in relation to these values that they hold as important.

Honor and shame are part of Chinese culture and impact the presentation and understanding of the gospel. Missiologist Jackson Wu presents the perspective that the gospel traditionally has been shared from a Western law-focused understanding of justification and atonement. He states that people who hear the gospel this way will need to think like Westerners in order to receive the message. Wu utilizes Chinese honor-shame based culture to demonstrate additional elements of truth and application in the Scriptures. He points to various Chinese theologians' perspectives on justification, demonstrating how honor and shame are cultural elements that provide key insights as to what God in Christ accomplished on the cross. He states:

> The message of the gospel within the Chinese cultural context should be characterized by the emphasis on honor, relationship, and harmony, which are at the core of traditional Chinese cultural values. It should be different from [traditional Western theology's] overemphasis on the forensic nature of the gospel, the legal dimension of Christ's penal substitution and divine justification. (2013, 27)

Chinese culture differs from Western individualism. Chinese identity and significance is tied to relationships with others. Personal shame or honor is directly related to one's relationship in bringing shame or honor to others, particularly family, and other significant persons who deserve one's respect. The impact of individual actions is also regarded as affecting the family's face, or honor and shame. "A person's identity consists in how others regard him or her. Face and identity arise both from one's network of relationships (ascribed honor-shame) and from individual actions (achieved honor-shame)" (2013, 294).

Therefore, it is important that the actions of God in regards to mankind, be understood from an honor-shame culture. Wu goes on to state:

> God seems to face a dilemma. To uphold his honor, he should justly inflict punishment upon all of sinful humanity. Yet, in his covenant with Abraham, God identified with mankind, attaching his name, via his promises, to the fate of all the nations. As they go, so goes the cosmic reputation of God. If he condemns sinful humanity, he would be unfaithful to his word. If God righteously keeps his promise regarding the nations, it would seem he forsakes justice and denies himself. This narrative provides the backdrop for Christ's atonement and justification.... A biblical view of the atonement underscores how Jesus glorifies his Father, "saving God's face" from the shame of his image bearers. Jesus restores honor to God's people, whose collective identity is in Christ. (2013, 183-4, 295)

In the communication of the gospel, it is important for the evangelist to be sensitive to the thinking of the Chinese culture. The gospel is for all people, and is not Western or Eastern, but from God. The missionary would be wise to have intentional interaction with Chinese to gain understanding regarding honor-shame culture. But we must understand that we plant and water but it is "God who makes it grow" (1 Cor. 3:6).

Philosophical Training of Chinese Scholars and Scientific Perspectives

Chinese scholars coming to America have been trained in the Chinese education system, and are part of the Chinese system, which includes atheistic belief and thought. "They have been influenced by 'scientific method,' Marxism, and traditional Chinese (including Confucian) values" (Ling 1999, 164).

The scientific mindset demands proof and discussions regarding the Bible and science. Chinese scholars are seeking truth to fill the spiritual void in their lives, but do so from a scientific perspective. Many scholars have come to faith through interaction with respected scientists, professors and professionals who share their belief in God with these seekers. All have a need for finding life's purpose and truth in the inner man.

In a study that Tso-Kung Chuang carried out among Chinese intellectual believers, his subjects stated that "finding inner strength," "finding direction for life," "peace of mind" and "finding the answer to life" became their motivation for their Christian conversion. As a consequence, they realized their obvious changes after conversion are "a greater inner joy," "clearer direction for life," and "more desire to serve others" (Wong 2006, 30).

Chapter 6

Love is the Key

The Importance of Christian Love and Care

Foreign Policy online featured an article titled "Leave China, Study in America, Find Jesus." The article shares stories of Chinese students who have come to the States to study and become Christians while they are here. Some are curious, some are hurting, some are seeking help, and some are seeking truth. All have been touched by someone in the United States who loves Jesus and has reached out and touched their lives.

This is our story as well. The opportunity is big with over 400,000 Chinese students at US universities and the effective instrument that God consistently uses to impact these lives with the gospel is loving relationships with Christians. This may include Christians welcoming Chinese students into their homes, helping them with English, caring for them in their struggles of adjusting to a different country, and just being there for them. Christians who demonstrate love, peace, joy, hope and the fruit of the Spirit are like a magnet to an empty heart.

The three most important words in sharing the gospel with Chinese students are Relationship, Relationship, and Relationship. This is

God's way. We see this clearly in these rhetorical questions in Romans 10:14-15: "How can they hear about him unless someone tells them? And how will anyone go and tell them without being sent?" (NLT) God uses loving relationships to bring those who are lost into his family. He uses relationships to bring people into the most important relationship of all.

When Christians are significantly present and develop caring relationships with the Chinese scholars in these times of adjustment, it impacts their openness to faith in Christ. Christian workers report that "Chinese intellectuals come to Christ most easily in the context of a caring community where their emotional, social, and spiritual needs are being met". Fenggang Yang points out that most Chinese conversions to Christianity in North America have been a result of "campus evangelical organizations and conservative Chinese churches and organizations".

Lai Fan Wong interviewed twelve Chinese scholars who became Christians after coming to America. All of them shared that a warm welcome from enthusiastic Christians drew them toward an interest in Christianity. They were impressed by a warmth, peace and joy that they saw in the lives of Christians. Bob Osburn reports that social support and practical assistance impact the responsiveness of the potential Christian convert. He cites the following pattern:

> (a) charitable, generous, and welcoming behavior; (b) non-coercive conversations about spiritual topics; (c) a practical focus on the felt needs of students, such as English conversation, airport pick-ups, personal counsel, and homestays; (d) sense of gratitude by the student; (e) respect and admiration for host(s); and (f) inquiry as to the rationale for assistance.

In Katie Rawson's surveys and interviews she stated that "people, Christian groups and individuals, were the most significant factors" in seeing people come to faith. The factors that attracted the students to the Christian groups were services offered, such as wanting to practice English, and the need for friendship. In particular, love was the attraction most frequently mentioned in the interviews. The good behavior of Christians was the second ranked attraction for seekers.

The Power of Love in Action

One Saturday my phone rang while I (Daniel) was playing with my 3-year-old son. I picked up the phone and it was the President of the Association of Chinese Students and Scholars. He told me he needed my help to provide an airport pickup at the Philadelphia airport the next day. He then chuckled saying "This is a family of four you're picking up. Daniel, to tell you the truth, if it were a single girl, our students would fight to get the opportunity to pick her up." I related the story to my wife Beth, saying "Now it's just dawned on me that I have never got a chance to pick up a female student!" She received my protest with a kind hug as if to comfort me — and I felt it.

Just as I was told, it was a family of four. This was their first visit in America. Bob Shi was a visiting scholar in his late 40s. He was already a very distinguished researcher in China in the field of alternative energy. He was doing research in Japan before coming to the US as a visiting scholar. He and his wife had two lovely kids — a four-year-old boy and a six-year-old girl. Together with their bags, they filled my good old Dodge Caravan. The sun was setting as we were going on Interstate 95. He was obviously an introvert and did not talk much. As we chatted on the way, I was surprised that they did not know anyone on the campus, and they did not have a dinner plan either. So, I called

Beth and asked her to prepare dinner for all of us.

At the dinner table at home, I prayed for the meal and thanked God for our new friends. So, they learned that we were a Christian family. I briefly shared how I became a Christian despite my atheist education and Buddhist family background in China. We enjoyed getting to know each other during the dinner time. Gradually, Bob was feeling more comfortable and was talking more. His wife Jan and Beth hit it off instantly. They talked about kids, school and cross-cultural experiences. The next day, I spent the whole day running errands on their behalf and helping them get registered with the school, do grocery shopping, and move into temporary housing.

It became apparent that Bob and Jan were very interested in making new friends. They were impressed by the many church buildings they saw wherever they went. I took them to the nearby Chinese church where they were warmly greeted. They also regularly attended our Friday Bible study group for students and professors, which was becoming like their family and home away from home. We did a lot of things together—going on trips out of town, celebrating holidays and our kids' birthdays, and inviting each other to dinners at home. We laughed and cried together. In the process, Bob and Jan came to realize that Christian believers were not as abnormal as they had expected, or as the Chinese propaganda would have painted them to be.

They found themselves admiring the kindness, humility and the joyful outlook on life they observed in Christians. At the same time, they began to show spiritual interests and asked good questions about God and the Bible. Two years after coming to America, they received Christ and were baptized. Even to this day, they are still walking with the Lord.

Looking back, I can see how Christian love and hospitality were helpful in opening their hearts and removing the prejudices they had about Christianity. Ultimately, they still had to examine and respond to the truth in the Christian message, but without the initial contact with loving Christians, they likely would have reacted negatively to any Christian claims.

Chapter 7

Coming to Faith in Christ: Inroads and Obstacles

What Chinese Scholars Say Influenced them to Become Christians

The factor mentioned most often on both the online and in person surveys regarding how Chinese scholars became a Christian is the involvement of Christians in their lives. This information is shown in Table 1. Many shared how they were welcomed by Christians in practical ways. Some had Christian roommates, and some were initially greeted and hosted by Christians when they arrived in America. Some were met at the airport and provided rides. Some scholars were hosted in the homes of Christians, either as temporary housing, or for meals and hospitality. One person said that they spent a lot of time with Christians, and another scholar said that the Christians "made him feel a part of their family." Others said they were touched by the love of Christians, and that Christians shared love and practical help and then shared the gospel. One scholar's observation was "I want to be like Christians to be able to love others." Some shared that they attended events for practical reasons, such as learning English, or having connections with other Chinese, but the caring love of the people created a desire in them for spiritual life.

The interviewees also mentioned that their observations of Christians played a key role in their coming to personal faith. Some mentioned they were attracted by the peace and joy of Christians, and also observed that Christians loved and lived in harmony with one another. Another shared that their roommate was a Christian and that they

Table 1: Top Answers to Survey Questions Regarding Influences to Become Christians		
Survey type:	Online	In person
	n = 40	n = 20
How did you become a Christian?		
1. Contact and influence of Christians	23 (58%)	16 (80%)
2. Involvement in the church	18 (45%)	7 (35%)
3. Coming to America	15 (38%)	9 (45%)
4. Involvement in a Bible study	10 (25%)	4 (20%)
5. Reading Bible personally	6 (15%)	3 (15%)
6. Sensing God is real/seeking Him	5 (13%)	5 (25%)
7. Difficulties	4 (10%)	3 (15%)
8. Books and resources	3 (8%)	1 (5%)
Why did you become a Christian?		
1. Choosing Truth	21 (53%)	6 (30%)
2. Desire for New Life	13 (33%)	8 (40%)
3. Respond to God's Call/Urging	8 (20%)	5 (25%)
4. Want to be like Christians they know	4 (10%)	4 (20%)
5. To be close to God	4 (10%)	0
6. Struggles/Difficulties	3 (8%)	2 (10%)
What did God use to impact your life and influence you to be a Christian?		
1. God's clear direction	23 (58%)	8 (40%)
2. Christians sharing	16 (40%)	8 (40%)
3. Answered Prayer	10 (25%)	2 (10%)
4. Love	6 (15%)	2 (10%)
5. Bible Studies/Reading Bible	5 (13%)	5 (25%)

observed joy in their life. Personal contact resulting in the opportunity to actually observe the life of those who are following Christ is a factor that scholars stated caused them to consider the gospel personally. One said their decision to follow Christ came through their direct interaction with God and people who are following God. They were touched to see the living testimony of love and faith. Some said that they could feel God's love in their contact times with Christians.

The interaction with Christians and the observation of their lives resulted in a desire among many interviewed to consider Christian faith. Several mentioned that they wanted what they observed. They wanted to have love, joy and peace in their own lives. A Post-Doctoral researcher said, "…they have something special. I want what they have." They went on to say, "I want to be like Christians to be able to love others…I want to have the joy that Christians have. I want to continue my faith journey even when I go back to China and help others in China to receive this peace and joy only Jesus can provide."

Observing the attitudes of Christians toward others and in facing life's difficulties was also stated as having an effect. A positive outlook on life, friendliness and kindness were observed. This observation created desire within the scholars to have this life for them. Commitment and sincerity were also mentioned as characteristics that were observed in Christians and impacted the scholars to consider personal faith.

The connections with Christians resulted in Chinese students and scholars attending events and programs. The church was the number one place where scholars were invited to attend or were taken to by a Christian friend. One scholar received temporary housing from a member of the Chinese church and was invited to church. She heard the gospel through several messages and small group Bible studies. Another scholar said that they wished to "improve their oral and listening English", went to the local church hosting English language classes, and this led to further involvement with the people that they met at the church. Many mentioned that they were introduced to, or met Christians who invited and took them to church with them, and they continued to attend resulting in them hearing the gospel.

Involvement with the church was the number two influence mentioned in response to how they became a Christian. A master's student said, "I went to church for the first time one day after I arrived in the US." A Ph.D. student said, "I was deeply attracted by the church life and the peace and joy the Christians had. I was also attracted by how they lived in harmony with one another." There were some who said that they were not interested in church, but did accept the invitation to go, and continued to attend. One went to the church because they were feeling great pressure in their studies and were looking for spiritual help. Many experienced the comfort of the care and prayers of others through the church, such as this scholar who shared: "I ran into some serious setbacks in life. The prayers by church friends offered me great emotional comfort and influence." The scholars were also invited to various programs, conferences and retreats by Christians and people they met in the church.

This Chinese scholar shares how the church fellowship was used by God to impact her life:

> When I arrived in the United States I had no friends. I felt very lonely and also needed help. Beside I thought America was a Christian nation. And I wanted to know about Christianity. So one day, I asked a colleague in our office, if there is a Christian church nearby. I was surprised when he said he is a Christian. He told me he can take me to Grace Fellowship. I still remember the

first time I went, everyone was very friendly, and this made me feel very warm.

In China I didn't know much about the Bible, and Christians. In Grace Fellowship, I thought everyone was very kind, friendly and always happy to help. This moved me very much. In the Bible study I learned a lot about God. I learned that he created everything. Also Jesus did many miracles like healing sick people. He can do this because he is God. These things impressed me very much. The most important thing is God loves us whether we are American or Chinese. I also learned that we are all sinners. Jesus paid the price for our sins when he died on the cross. On the third day Jesus arose from the dead, this proves he is God.

One day my colleague and a girl from Grace Fellowship came to my home, the girl explained how to become a Christian, then she asked me if I wanted to receive Jesus. I answered yes. Then they prayed for me, and then I prayed to receive Christ.

Before I received Christ I felt that my heart was empty because I had no faith. I thought work is the most important thing in life, this gave me a lot of pressure because I wanted to be promoted. To get promoted is very difficult. Working hard for promotion made me very tired every day. Sometimes at home I would be very irritable, and this made my home very unhappy, and I found this is very painful. I didn't realize that it was my fault that my home was unhappy. I often blamed my family. I almost wanted to divorce my husband.

The biggest difference after I received Christ is that I can handle the pressure now. I can tell God about my problem, and sometimes he will help me solve the problems, and sometimes he just gives me peace about them. So I don't get angry easily with my family anymore. For example, recently my husband got to visit here for a month and a half. Our relationship was much better than before. Another difference is that my heart is no longer empty, and I am very glad to be a member of God's family. And the most important thing is God loves us.

Coming to America — Forever Changed

The third highest element of impact mentioned was coming to America. Many mentioned it in their answer to the question in a "matter of fact" way but definitely included it as a significant element in their coming to faith. One said "I knew that this country [the United States] was free to talk and to learn about Jesus. So I wanted to come here." Some were very specific as one who said, "I felt that I traveled thousands of miles to America, and on top of that, to come to know Christ." Another said, "Since childhood I had believed there was a god, and I had always seriously wanted to find him. I had encountered different religions and had some church life in China. However, true change occurred after coming to America." Moving from a culture where any belief or faith was not encouraged, and even discouraged, to a culture where there is freedom to believe seems to have opened the door for many. One scholar shared: "I did not believe in any religion in China but became a Christian two years after coming to America."

Bible studies and Christian fellowships were also mentioned many times as elements that led the Chinese to become a Christian. At these gatherings, the interviewees mentioned that they continued to observe the Christians interacting with them and with each other. Many said they were impressed with how the Christians loved one another and were giving toward others. At the church and Bible studies, they began to hear and understand the message of salvation and the truth of God's Word. "I started to read Bible with help of Christians and I gradually understood God's words. I believe that God's words are true." Some said that they had direct contact with the pastor and were impacted by the pastor's teaching and counsel.

Choosing Truth

The number one answer as to why they became a Christian was a choice for truth. Forty-five percent of all surveyed gave this as a part of their answer to this question. One scholar said, "I sought for answers in other religions too and felt lonely deep within me and did not find what to trust. But God can listen to my prayer any time." Many wrestled as scientists with the compatibility of faith with science, particularly the topic of evolution. One said, "Since truth is not to be changed because of our belief or unbelief, none of us can argue against or avoid the fact that Jesus was crucified for the sins of man and was resurrected three days later." And another said, "After studying Genesis and checking with scientific facts I reconciled with the fact that there is a God." Some said the message of the Bible made sense to them and others shared that they studied carefully the teachings of the Bible and realized that they never would understand everything, but they could take action by faith on what they did understand. Some reflected on how they had an awareness of God even early in life, and when they began to read the Bible and hear the gospel, they realized that this was the true God that they had desired to know. The relief and peace that this brought is reflected in one scholar's statement: "It felt good to finally get to know this God to whom I've been praying."

This testimony illustrates one who sought after truth and found it in Christ:

> I came to US from China and journeyed across borders: geographical, linguistic, social and intellectual. I expected a new gate to be opened in front of me, but never realized I could have been so lucky to cross from a life of perplexed darkness to the realm filled with bright benevolent redemption.
>
> What did my life look like before Christ?
>
> I used to live a life with perplexities: Unable to recall since when a few fundamental questions had kept recurring to me :
>
> • What is the meaningfulness of me living in this world?
> • How should I deal with another person when we have conflicts?
> • Why do people bitterly hate one another and even mercilessly slaughter one another?
> • What does it mean by living in such an indifferent world?
>
> I used to seek truth of life and like many others, I failed. I failed to find it in Confucius doctrines or in intellectual study. Long time puzzlement resulted in my pretending to forget it, pretending those questions never haunted my mind. To me, this world had no purpose; my living in this world made no difference other than to my family. I lived my life intuitively, in a habitual way, doing routine jobs like many others. Let's use cars to make comparison; I felt as if I were merely a toy car, moving forward just because of being wound up, instead of a powerful car which knows clearly and exactly where to go and how to reach there.

That was me. However, it is not who I am now. Now one person, and at the same time one God, Lord Jesus appears in the front and takes me by hand, saying "I am the way and the truth and the life." Now it suddenly dawns upon me that he knows me! My existence does make sense—he cares about me! He allowed himself to be killed in a bloody, painful, humiliated way 2000 years ago in order for me to understand today that he actually cares about me. On my way I received his profound love; presently I accept him as my Savior in life and appreciate that he has made all the perplexity lifted on my road ahead:

1. In his eyes I make a difference;
2. He created this world, and his love is constantly here. He shed his blood onto the ground. His blood is with temperature and it warms this world;
3. The reason why people have conflicts and hatred and slaughter is that human beings have fallen in dreadful sin by foolishly putting oneself instead of God in the center;
4. The meaningfulness of me standing on this earth consists in living a life like God and glorify HIM and helping more people to know him.

The second highest answer to "why I became a Christian" was a desire for a new or changed life. Thirty-five percent of all surveyed mentioned this in some form. Some mentioned that they tried to change their life, or wanted to change, and continued to find it impossible to do so and that this desire to change led them to consider trusting Jesus to change them. Another said, "Many years of my college life in China was not a happy memory. I recalled how selfish I was, seeking my own interests. I kept climbing up my ladder for the sake of my own survival and my own ambition. When I had the opportunity to learn about the gospel, I realized I could have a new life and that the only trust is to trust in the Lord to live rather than trust in myself…Rather I want to be a new self, learning to love other people and to receive love from others. Thus I can now humble myself and be myself and full of joy." Eight also said that they responded to God's call. Many said they sensed that God loved them and they realized that the message of the gospel was the truth.

The third question that was asked was "What did God use to impact your life and influence you to be a Christian?" God's clear direction was the top answer. This information is shown in Table 1. One Ph.D. shared, "God put that desire inside of me, I totally changed from an 8-year Party member to a Christian, I sometimes don't believe this change could happen to me." Another said that they strongly felt God's power as they observed the natural world. The sharing of Christians was something observed as God at work. Some actually said that God sent Christians into their lives. Another said that it was through the love and faith of Christians that they could feel God's love. Answered prayer and provision for needs was the third most mentioned factor of God impacting their lives. One said that during difficult moments, "God opened the door showing his love and plan to me. I have to believe that God is looking for me and showing his power and faithfulness to me." One person mentioned a dream and healing experience, and another mentioned miracles taking place.

The Role of Relationships with Christian Workers

The survey asked questions regarding the impact of Christian workers in three different ways. First was how Christian workers encouraged the Chinese scholar to become a Christian. Second was how Christian workers impeded the scholar's process to become a Christian. And third was how Christian workers helped them overcome faith obstacles. The responses to these questions will be considered in this section.

The surveys indicated a strong positive response by Chinese students and scholars regarding the positive impact of Christian workers in their coming to a personal faith in Christ. This information is shown in Table 2. The Christian workers' presence seems to be the key factor seen in these answers. Christian workers were there for them and with them in their faith pilgrimage. Their personal testimony and evidence of life transformation was the number one influence given by Chinese scholars surveyed (43%). As mentioned in an earlier section, the scholars were impacted by seeing and sensing something in the lives of believers that resulted in a personal desire for that difference. Words such as friendly, sincere, loving, peaceful, joyful, embracing, and encouraging appear many times. One scholar commented, "I could tell by the positive attitude toward life (I didn't know if it was cultural or faith) but the openness and welcoming smiles made me

Table 2: Influence of Christian Workers on Belief of Chinese Scholars

Survey type:	Online n = 40	In person n = 20
What roles in the lives of Christian workers encouraged you to be a Christian?		
1. Testimony/Changed Lives	18 (45%)	12 (67%)
2. Care and Love	17 (43%)	7 (35%)
3. Selfless Help	13 (33%)	2 (10%)
4. Encouragement/No Pressure	8 (20%)	3 (15%)
5. Answered Questions/Teaching	7 (18%)	6 (30%)
6. Joyful/Happy Life	7 (18%)	2 (10%)

sure some of this was from God as well as cultural." Another said, "I am impressed by the attitude of their everyday life, the attitude when they are confronted of difficulty. Also, they are always willing to help others." One scholar gave a direct reference as to how the testimony of changed lives resulted in her conversion: "Other Christians' testimony and their new life in Christ encourage me to be a Christian." As one scholar put it, "From them I saw the image of Jesus Christ. Without them I could not know God."

The second most given answer is closely related to the first, but was specific to what was experienced; Christians showed care and love (40%). The scholars found this attractive and were encouraged to continue to seek personal faith. One scholar said, "They gave me the kind of love this world and society could not give." Another said, "Their selfless love and care was something I never saw in China." The love of Christians demonstrated the love of God to the scholars as noted in this statement: "I felt loved and God's power in their faith journey, their knowledge of Christ and selfless devotion."

The third highest answer was selfless help. This included receiving practical help, giving time, listening, and generosity. A thirty-two year old female Master's student shared: "They were very giving and did not complain. They were sincere to everyone and selflessly offered help. To me these are the ideal people I had never met in life. As a result I desired to live a Christian life and to be like them." Another shared, "Their generosity and unselfishness caused me to seek the true source of this unfailing river of kindness to the unlovely people like us, asking what energy source powered this fountain of gentleness?" Again, the personal interaction and care was a factor in causing this scholar to consider Christian faith for themselves: "Being kind and generous. I wanted to be like they are, devoted to God. They served

God, took me to church, helped me study in Sunday School, answered questions, and gave me the book *More than a Carpenter.*"

Encouragement without pressure, teaching and giving answers to questions, and a joyful and happy life were the next three items mentioned by scholars to this question. The issue of pressure shows up later in the study under the question related to Christian workers impeding their considering Christianity. It is stated as appreciated when there was freedom to think without pressure, and was stated as negative when that pressure was felt. One said, "they always encourage me but never push me." Being there for them in need without pressure was a key element as seen in this comment: "The person comforted me when I was having a tough time and prayed for me." Answering questions and giving them helpful Bible teaching was also appreciated and a help in their process. "They patiently helped me with the questions I had and prayed for me when I had difficulties in life." "They found answers to many questions I had about the Bible." Joy and happiness in the lives of Christian workers made an impression upon the scholars and aided in their consideration of faith. "The love they shared with me in a practical way moved me, and let me think why they could be different from people who were not Christians. Other good examples were: the peace and joy of Christians they demonstrated despite of their illness and suffering." "They lived a life that was fully alive with a joyful life outlook, and their heart that truly loved the Lord."

The following testimony of a Ph.D. student demonstrates the impact of a Christian worker in the process of coming to faith in Christ:

The turning point in my belief started at the intellectual level. In the third year of my Ph.D. study, I took classes on European intellectual history in the 17th and 18th centuries, which is a period of intense debate on the nature of God and Scripture. The materials I read in these classes prompted me to seriously reflect on the existence of God and his plan of salvation. Theoretically, the idea of an omnipotent Creator, who not only lays out the natural order but also cares for the welfare of each individual, gave me great comfort. Furthermore, the widespread violence, cruelty and injustice in the human world can be easily explained given the fallen state of man.

What drew me even closer to God, however, was the series of strikes in my personal life. The setbacks in my academic life, the outbreak of my migraine headaches and the death of my father gave me one strike after another. Eventually I lost all passion and motivation, becoming listless, helpless and hopeless. Almost out of desperation, I decided to find a church, hoping to change my situation through asking for help from the God I somehow knew of. I started to attend Sunday worship and was introduced to a fellowship group designed mainly for Chinese visiting scholars and students.

To my surprise, I found that the Bible study was taught by an American pastor, whose teaching I very much enjoyed. What impressed me most, however, was how approachable and sensitive he was to my spiritual needs. Different from many other members who were being introduced to the Christian faith for the first time, I had a definite purpose when I joined the fellowship group. My purpose was to establish an intimate relationship with God and to have him as my friend, comforter and counselor in the most difficult period of my life. One day in the discussion, I raised the question of how one could establish a personal relationship with God. Afterward, our Pastor Teacher approached me and asked if I could meet with him for further discussion. We talked in the library for over an hour. His sincerity and eagerness to offer help deeply impressed me, and I told him about my struggle. During that talk, he showed me the verse from Psalm 131, which says, "But I have stilled and quieted my soul; like a weaned child with its mother." The state described in the psalm—that peace, rest and assurance from knowing and trusting in God—was exactly what I needed at that time.

I longed for such a state, but was I hesitant about opening my heart completely to accept Christ as my Savior, perhaps because my first decision to get baptized was a quick and impulsive one. This time I wanted to wait until I was one-hundred-percent sure. In the two years after my first talk with the Pastor, during which I continued to pursue a personal relationship with God in my own way, Christians I knew continued to interact with me, patiently answering my questions, offering care and support. The Pastor also encouraged me to consistently participate in church activities and to interact more with other church members.

Months later, I finally realized that it is my own sin of pride, and my willfulness to go my own way that prevented me from accepting Jesus Christ as my Savior and the Lord of my life. Following our leader's advice, I decided to be baptized for the second time to declare true faith in Christ. After years of struggle and detour, I came to a true understanding of the value of God's love for me and the meaning of his salvation for me.

Although most everyone surveyed listed positive things about Christian workers and their influence, many did not list any negative statements. The question was asked, "Were there factors in the lives of

Table 3: Factors in the Lives of Christian Workers that Impeded the Process of Becoming a Christian		
Survey type:	Online n = 40	In person n = 20
1. None/nothing	19 (48%)	7 (35%)
2. Complaining, Criticizing, Judging, Condemning, Not getting along	7 (18%)	4 (20%)
3. Bad behavior/questionable commitment	5 (13%)	4 (20%)
4. Pushy, high pressure with Gospel	4 (10%)	4 (20%)

Christian workers that impeded your progress in becoming a Christian?" Forty-eight percent of the online survey participants said there were none, and thirty-five percent of those surveyed in person also said there was nothing. This information is shown in Table 3. Many said they realized that no one was perfect and even though they were at times disappointed, it didn't discourage them.

The items that were mentioned as impeding fit into three categories: complaining, criticizing, judging, condemning, or not getting along; bad behavior and questionable commitment; and feeling pushed or pressured with the gospel. Attitudes, behavior and evangelism practice summarize these three areas.

It is evident that the Chinese scholar who is considering faith is watching the behavior of Christian workers and responds to what they see and feel. One mentioned that the way they had been taught history and things they had heard about Christians had been negative.

Obstacles to Responding to the Gospel and the Role Others Play in Helping Overcome These Obstacles

We asked the Chinese scholars: "What were the personal, cultural, or relational obstacles that you had to overcome before you could make the decision to become a Christian?" and "What role did Christians

Table 4: Obstacles Faced by Scholars in Becoming Christians		
Survey type:	Online n = 40	In person n = 20
1. Chinese Culture/Communistic Atheism	15 (38%)	7 (35%)
2. Returning to China, Party Member	8 (20%)	2 (10%)
3. Family Members (Parents)	7 (18%)	7 (35%)
4. Science and Christianity (Evolution)	1 (3%)	5 (25%)

play in helping to overcome these obstacles?" The results are shown in Table 4.

The number one obstacle shared was overcoming the cultural differences between communistic atheism and what the scholars were hearing shared by Christians in America. The struggle was really one of what is true and what to believe in. The scholars had to reevaluate what they had been taught throughout their lives. The belief that there is no God, that all that exists is what we can see, and that all we can believe in is ourselves, were big obstacles to overcome. The second highest obstacle was being a Communist Party member. To be a member of the Party one promises not to have any religious beliefs and Party membership is a key element in moving forward in one's position. The third highest obstacle given is a concern regarding the response and thoughts of parents and of other family members. All of these seem to flow from the same basic issue: the concern for respect for cultural traditions, for family and for prior commitments. One of the scholars surveyed gave this comment: "I had to overcome my own growth experiences, social and cultural issues, and family upbringing because these issues contributed to my own identity." There is also a fear factor involved since returning to China as a Christian could impact one's job and career.

Atheistic teaching and the cultural influence that forms the belief and mindset of the Chinese scholar is a stumbling block. One scholar said, "The greatest obstacle is the atheistic brainwashing in China, and the current multi-culturalism is also an obstacle because it makes one feel that Christian faith after all is only one of the many cultures."

Another shared: "The key thing for me was to transition from atheism to theism. Once I believed there was a God, all other issues did not present themselves to be a challenge to me." It seems that this is a major step in the process of true saving faith. The first step of faith is to believe that there is a God.

One scholar stated: "Due to our school system, I was brought up as a materialistic atheist and that was an obstacle in my faith journey. It made me to think that only the visible is real. So regarding this invisible God only through belief would I get to see him." This rationalistic thinking is also mentioned by this scholars answer: "My education since childhood formed my mentality of "self-reliance and self-strength." Therefore it was hard for me to trust myself in God's hand. My rational thinking has made it difficult to get into a personal relationship with God." Another scholar focused on the history of the Communist Party for their masters and Ph.D. and were totally immersed in Marxism. They stated, "I was raised as an atheist with the typical communist education background. I never had believed there is God, as the song *The International* goes: 'There are no supreme saviors, neither God, nor Caesar, Let us save ourselves'. I firmly believed that our future is in our own hand by working hard, getting good education and good jobs. So my education background often affected me. It's difficult for me to overcome this one."

The second highest response is the impact of returning to China as a Christian and the dynamic impact of being a Communist Party member. One scholar shared that the "issue is the prospect of return-ing to China. If I tell others that I'm a Christian, that would likely get me into some troubles." Another said, "My parents are both very committed Communist Party members, I myself am a Party member, and my fiancé currently serves in China's military." And the issue of fear of the government was clearly expressed by this scholar's answer: "Fear of my government. You have no idea how scared I was! In China you have no right to have your religion."

The third highest response was the concern for the response of family members as well as friends. The Chinese culture seems to place a great emphasis on honoring parents and saving face for the person and their family. To go against the wishes and ideals of parents is very negative. Therefore, to make a decision of personal faith in Christ when that goes against the parents' wishes and desires is a great struggle. One of the struggles mentioned was the idea of being separated from family after death if they don't believe as shared by this scholars answer: "None of my family members are Christians. According to Christian doctrines, we can't be united after death. This makes me feel sad. I hope they will come to believe in the Lord later on."

Christian faith verses science and evolution was mentioned as an obstacle by one-fourth of those surveyed in person. One shared that they had been taught that anyone who believed that we were cre-ated was stupid, and that people believe in religion because they are uneducated. Another said, "In China I was told by the government evolution was science and the truth. Christianity was superstition."

The culture, the Party, and family are all a part of the identity of Chinese students and scholars. This scholar expressed this well: "First, coming from an atheistic culture might be the primary obstacle which includes the education I got, relatives and friends I have. Secondly, I

Table 5: Help From Christian Workers in Overcoming Obstacles		
Survey type:	Online n = 40	In person n = 20
1. Shared their lives/testimonies	22 (55%)	10 (50%)
2. Answered Questions/Teaching	12 (30%)	8 (20%)
3. Shared God's Word/Bible Study	8 (20%)	4 (20%)
4. Friendship/Love/Encouragement	8 (20%)	5 (25%)
5. Prayer	5 (13%)	2 (5%)

have troubles when facing ancestor worship, which is also common in Chinese families." The concept of ancestor worship was mentioned by a few and is a specific family and cultural issue for those who become Christians. When one returns to China, they must face these cultural realities as a Christian. The scholars' awareness of this struggle is an obstacle in making a faith decision.

Those surveyed were also asked how Christian workers helped them in overcoming these obstacles. The majority stated that the sharing by Christian workers of their own experiences, their struggles, and their own testimonies of coming to faith helped in the struggle with obstacles. This information is shown in Table 5. One scholar said that her Chinese Christian roommate and others shared their struggles about believing and this was a help to her. The presence of Christians and the evidence of a transformed life was impactful.

"Some of the American Christians were very helpful and influential. Very helpful. Good friends. Important. Why were these Christians so nice, so helpful, so consistently? There was something different. This would never happen in China! Why do they spend so much time with students—without pay! I'm really curious. I want to be more like them."

Long-term friendship and walking together through life occur-
rences was shared as a key element of help. "I met with a COM worker
for 5 years every Friday morning starting as a unbeliever. His life and
love impress me a lot, and he helped me a lot through his prayer and
long-time friendship." Another said that Christian workers "were all
sincere. So that encouraged me to become more interested in God's
word." And another said it very succinctly, identifying the help as
"their own life examples."

The second highest help from Christian workers to overcome
obstacles was answering questions and teaching. This was not formal
teaching but was personal sharing, and specific application to the persons' concerns. "They helped me know Christian faith and answered
some questions I had when reading the Bible." "They teach me more
about the relationship between God and myself." "They answered
my questions using scientific knowledge, sometimes they used their
own example to show me how their questions were solved. It is very
helpful to be around people who are willing to share and to witness."
The personal connection was clearly helpful and appreciated. "They
patiently help me and helped me know the truths."

Sharing God's Word in Bible study, friendship, love, encouragement, and prayer were other elements mentioned that were received
and found helpful by the scholars in their times of wrestling with
obstacles. One scholar shared that they were encouraged to trust God
even in the midst of the obstacles: "They told me don't worry about
these obstacles since they are common. God has his time. I can remain
still knowing it is in God's hand."

The students and scholars were also asked if there were obstacles
that were actually created by Christian workers that impeded their
pilgrimage to faith in Christ. Most that were surveyed said that there

were none that they experienced. Just over twenty percent shared that bad behavior and question of character were exhibited and observed among Christian workers. This information is shown in Table 6. Again, it did seem that some of the answers were more pointed to Christians in general rather than to just Christian workers. The most concerning bad behavior mentioned was a married man who was showing inappropriate attention to a Chinese coed. Other behaviors mentioned included betraying confidential information, "accuse, create trouble and pass judgments", "not loving each other" and one said "some Christians don't behave well outside the church."

The other area mentioned in the surveys was too much pressure applied to respond to the gospel. One shared an experience of someone who "kept quoting the Bible in wrong circumstances." Another said, "They were over-zealous and even appeared to be interfering with my private life." One scholar said some workers were not really concerned for her real needs but just wanted to share the gospel. In one of the in-person interviews, the interviewer recorded this inappropriate event: "When she first came, a group of Christians from a Chinese church helped her and then within a week came to her apartment to share the gospel. (She wasn't interested because she thought they had helped her just so they could share the gospel with her; they had not built a relationship with her first.) Then they started singing worship songs

Table 6: Obstacles Created by Christian Workers		
Survey type:	Online n = 40	In person n = 20
1. None	18 (45%)	14 (70%)
2. Bad behavior/character	9 (23%)	4 (20%)
3. Pushy/over zealous	2 (5%)	1 (5%)

in her apartment. She thought that was really weird." The concept of pressing too much, too quickly was shared. Giving enough time to process the information and for the Spirit to move them personally was a need expressed.

Chapter 8

Evangelism is a Process

Necessity and Importance of Articulating the Christian Message

People may have their first encounter with the Christian faith in different ways and then go through a process before a true conversion. Whatever the process, eventually, truth encounter is indispensable and critically important. This is especially true for Chinese students and scholars.

All students in China go through atheistic indoctrination during the middle and high school years as required by the government and enforced by the school system. They are taught materialism as a philosophy. Matter is the fundamental substance in all that exists, and all reality — visible or invisible — is material in nature and a result of material interactions. In holding this view, one logically rules out the possibility for a spiritual realm. There is no room left for gods, spirits, demons or ghosts.

Even if atheism and materialistic philosophy were true, they offer no hope, meaning, or consolation to the human heart. Therein lies the Achilles heel for atheism. In contrast, Christians proclaim the risen

Savior, in whom is love, meaning, purpose, strength for the present and hope for eternal life. To us it seems obvious that anyone in their right mind would choose to believe the Christian message. But would they?

This is a key component to why Christianity is attractive to the Chinese — if they get a chance to understand Christianity as it is or to meet Christians. The attraction is even greater for the Chinese students and scholars coming to study in America. This is true for several reasons: First, they have a need for social life when they come to a new country. Second, as newcomers, they need people who are kind, patient and trustworthy to help them get established, and Christians are just the right people to fill this need. Third, Chinese tend to desire assimilation into the new culture, to learn the new cultural norms, and to be accepted by people around them. They know America has a strong Christian heritage and learning about Christianity is part of learning about America.

Many Christians ministering to international students have noted that those who appear to be most interested in the Christian message and Christian activities often come from atheist countries like China. It is encouraging to see Chinese coming to outreach activities such as a welcome party or Bible study, but we should not always take it to mean that they are spiritually interested. Their interests could be partially or mostly cultural.

Many of those who have professed to be Christian and returned to China are not continuing on with their faith. This has led to much discussion among Christian workers as to the cause and how we may need to do ministry differently. One caution we all seem to agree on is that we need to be discerning before proclaiming a Chinese as a new believer. In a discussion, a group of Christian returnees to China were asked to reflect on the subject of why so many "Christians" do not continue in their faith after they return to China. We came to conclude that many of these "Christians" were likely never truly converted in America to start with!

A True Conversion?

What typically happens to a Chinese is that, soon after coming to America, he begins to interact with Christians and finds them to be very kind. In China, strangers do not take initiatives to get to know each other, but Christians do. They are loving and helpful; they care about his life and study; they take him grocery shopping during the weekends; they help him move when his lease runs out; they come and help when he has an argument with his wife; they give him tips about how to raise kids in America; they invite him to their home for dinner. In the process they also take him to church, where he meets many nice and friendly people and hears Christian messages. As a result, he really admires them and wishes to be like them. He is so touched by their love and kindness that when asked if wants to become a Christian, he says yes and prays with them. After that, they baptize him.

So the question is: is this person truly converted in God's eyes? Obviously, it depends. He is not a true convert if he was merely touched by the love of Christians and wanted to be like them. However, he is a true convert if the complete gospel message was presented and understood—if he had sorrow for his sin, wanted to repent and live a new life, realized his need for redemption, put his faith in Christ and accepted him as his Savior and Lord.

While love and hospitality is a demonstration of God's love and it can help to point unbelieving hearts toward God, it can also become a distraction from the gospel message. Christian hospitality is not a substitute for a clear presentation of the complete gospel. Not only does the message need to be well presented by the Christian worker, but it also needs to be well understood and grasped by the nonbeliever. Otherwise the response, positive or negative, would be meaningless. This is a huge challenge for the Christian presenting the gospel, particularly if this involves cross-cultural communication in a second language. I (Daniel) feel that Christian workers may not be doing due diligence in presenting the gospel well. We may be tempted to think that God's Spirit is at work and he will take care of it. While it is true that the Spirit is at work, we need to be faithful in doing our part to communicate truth.

True conversion occurs when the nonbeliever responds to the love of Christ; a false conversion occurs when he responds instead to the love of Christians. A truth encounter is necessary! For a true conversion to occur, it needs to take place in the heart, the mind, and the will. It is the truth, not feelings, that will set him free.

The importance of emphasizing truth is confirmed by a survey conducted by Dr. Zuotao Li. He was a graduate of Beijing University, came to the US for his Ph.D. and became a Christian through the work of China Outreach Ministries. He conducted this survey among believers in a predominantly ethnically Chinese church made up of mostly well-educated new immigrants from China. About 90% of the adult members hold postgraduate degrees. Forty-eight of them participated in the survey. The survey questions, shown in Table 7, were designed to identify key factors impacting an unbelieving educated Chinese' faith journey.

As the survey shows, the highest priority is on truth—whether spiritual truth or scientific truth. After all, all truth is God's truth. How Christians present, or fail to present, truth makes a significant difference—positively or negatively—in their faith journey.

Table 7: Survey Questions and Results

Question 1: Why did you want to become a Christian?

(Choose one)

1. Christian teaching (Bible) is the truth	18 (37.5%)
2. Have a new and eternal life	8 (16.7%)
3. Christianity has a better explanation on human nature and sin	7 (14.6%)
4. Need help in personal struggles or difficulties	6 (12.5%)
5. Christianity contributes positively in the society and Christians have higher moral values because of their faith	4 (8.3%)
6. God will bless me to be more successful	3 (6.3%)
7. Christianity is the most respected, mainstream religion in America	2 (4.2%)

Question 2: What was the primary obstacle for you in becoming a Christian?

(Choose one)

1. Conflict with science, anti-intellectual and anti-scientific	18 (37.5%)
2. Conflict with Chinese culture or atheist belief	14 (29.2%)
3. No chance to have a better understanding of Christian faith	10 (21%)
4. Its unsatisfactory explanation of human suffering with a loving God	3 (6.3%)
5. It is a tool for political powers	2 (4.1%)
6. The unacceptable or difficult teaching in the Bible, e.g. Original Sin, Hell, etc.	1 (2.1%)
7. Its exceedingly narrow, legalistic view of morality	0 (0%)

The Path to Conversion and Faith for the Typical Chinese

For a long time I (Daniel) kept narrowly focusing on proclaiming the gospel message to non-Christians without much positive results until one day it dawned on me that evangelism was a process, not a moment in time. When I was studying at Liberty Baptist Theological Seminary in 1991, in my research I was very excited to come across the decision-making process that Dr. James Engel outlined to describe the

Engel Scale — Spiritual Decision Process

Stage	Key Indicators
-8	Awareness of Supreme Being, no knowledge of Gospel
-7	Initial awareness of Gospel
-6	Awareness of fundamentals of Gospel
-5	Grasp implications of Gospel
-4	Positive attitude towards Gospel
-3	Personal problem recognition
-2	Decision to act
-1	Repentance and faith in Christ
+	New birth
+1	Post-decision evaluation
+2	Incorporation into Body
+3	Conceptual and behavioral growth
+4	Communion with God
+5	Stewardship

Source: J.F. Engel and W.H. Norton, *What's Gone Wrong With the Harvest?*

steps a non-Christian typically must go through in coming to faith. However, when I applied that process to a Chinese person, I ran into a problem. Dr. Engel's starting point in the conversion process was an "awareness of Supreme Being but no Effective Knowledge of Gospel." A typical educated Chinese, however, has little to no awareness of the Supreme Being due to the atheistic indoctrination in China's education system. They often do not seem to care about what happens after life. Even if they are aware of their sins or moral failures—so what?

I felt I needed to come up with a new chart to describe the extra hurdles the Chinese need to overcome before coming to know Christ. Before an educated Chinese progresses to become aware of a supreme being, he has to deal with his negative attitudes toward the Christian faith, as the modified chart shows. It typically takes a longer process for a Chinese to truly commit himself to Christ. Based on my observation, when coming to America, most Chinese start at -6 where they have little or no awareness of the supreme being. Some of them have even more spiritual hurdles to overcome if they exhibit indicators associated with stages -7 to -9.

Typical Process for a Chinese Person Prior to Conversion

Stage	Key Indicators
-9	Hostility toward Christians
-8	Bias against or contempt for Christian faith
-7	Atheistic attitude or belief in other religions
-6	Little or no awareness of Supreme Being
-5	Some awareness of Supreme Being
-4	Open to Christian faith
-3	Interested in Christian faith
-2	Appreciate Christian values, Christians, or churches
-1	Understand the basics about the Gospel
+	*Moment of Conversion: Begin a new life in Christ!*
+1	Grow in Christ (a transformation process)
+2	Become mature

Implications for ministry to the Chinese

First, it is important that we, as Christian workers, are patient in helping our Chinese friends go through this process. Despite our wish to see them come to know Christ right away, we need to recognize this is a process they need to go through and it cannot be rushed. If a Chinese friend does not even believe God exists, to have him pray the sinner's prayer is meaningless. Rushing them through this process may make a good story in the newsletter, but it does not lead to a genuine conversion. And it is not God-honoring.

Second, this chart can help us become more sensitive to the hurdles our Chinese friend may be dealing with at the moment. If he has progressed to Stage -3, we do not need to spend time addressing the issue of atheism. Instead, we need to help him understand what the gospel message is all about.

Third, we can be encouraged that very likely our Chinese friend has made tremendous progress spiritually, as from moving forward from Stage -6 to Stage -4, even though he has not yet come to faith. We have already helped him come closer to Christ! We have already been used by God to make a difference in his life! Most of the time, God seems to only give us a chance to help a non-believer in part of the journey but not the whole journey. In fact, that is what the Bible teaches: "I planted the seed, Apollos watered it, but God has been making it grow. So neither the one who plants nor the one who waters is anything, but only God, who makes things grow. The one who plants and the one who waters have one purpose, and they will each be rewarded according to their own labor" (1 Cor. 3: 6-8). Indeed, God rarely gives us an opportunity to run the whole nine yards.

Finally, understanding the process can help us to stay humble when we get a chance to lead a Chinese student to Christ. That could be when he or she moves forward from stage -2 to the moment of conversion. It is important to stay humble knowing we are building on the ministry of other Christians who helped overcome spiritual hurdles in the past along this person's faith journey. Ultimately, we know it is the Holy Spirit alone who works in the heart to bring about new birth.

Elements of Christian Conversion

Jesus made it clear for his followers to "go and make disciples of all nations" (Matt. 28:19). Jesus goes on to tell us the parts of the process we are to do, which includes "baptizing them in them in the name of the Father and of the Son and of the Holy Spirit, and teaching them to obey everything I have commanded you". If we are to follow this command and to make disciples among the Chinese students and scholars, it is helpful to understand the elements involved in a person coming to a point of Christian conversion, or actually becoming a disciple of Jesus Christ.

Lewis R. Rambo has done definitive research in the area of religious conversion. He defines seven stages in the conversion process: context, crisis, quest, encounter, interaction, commitment and consequences. He states that "conversion takes place within a dynamic context...it is the total environment in which conversion transpires". The context is both external and internal and shapes the process of conversion for each person. It includes social, cultural, religious, and personal dimensions.

Robert Osburn's research on Christian conversion among international students reflects on Rambo's findings and uncovers six themes: social support and practical assistance from US Americans; incorporation into a community of Christians; honest, critical inquiry; paradigm-transforming events; validity markers and enhanced spirituality. He also cites Stark's theory of conversion which considers migration a major factor leading to conversion, because newcomers must make new friends.

There are a variety of other ingredients that are related to individuals coming to Christ. George Houssney interviewed many Muslims who converted and recorded several additional factors, including the love of Christians, and dreams and visions.

Charles Kraft identifies five constants in biblical conversion: a conscious allegiance to God; dynamic interaction springing from this allegiance; growth or maturation; the need for commitment and maturation to occur in community; and the need for the conversion process to occur in keeping with the culture in which converts are immersed. Kraft also states that allegiance, truth and power encounters are each necessary for effective Christian witness; an integration of the three is needed for a total approach to Christian ministry.

Richard Peace reflects on Paul's conversion and the conversion of the disciples as recorded in the book of Mark to discover what is different and what is similar. The difference, he finds, is mainly related to time—Paul's conversion was rather quick, while the process for the disciples took a longer period of time. Peace notes that there are specific characteristics that are present in every conversion—including insight, turning, and transformation—but that that the process is unique to each individual. "What was an event for Paul," he says, "is described by Mark as a process for the Twelve".

Peace makes a case for process evangelism and gives suggestions and guidelines. It is coming alongside others who need Christ in love and without judgment, discovering where they are in their spiritual journey, and being there to help guide them toward a relationship with Jesus. Process evangelism involves developing in-depth relationships with unbelievers, and allowing Christ to demonstrate his transforming power in our lives. It is one sinner who has come to know the love of God and his forgiveness, sharing their life with another so they too may know.

> There is no "us and them" any longer. Both those who are committed to Christ and those who are coming to Christ are challenged by the words of Jesus. Both are called to respond to Jesus in terms of where they are in their own spiritual pilgrimages. (1999, 320)

Scott McKnight agrees that the conversion process is unique for each individual. "Conversion means something personal to each convert," he says, "and its manifestations vary according to the personality with its history and needs." He lists six reasons for conversion: to find pleasure or to avoid pain; to embrace an intellectually satisfying conceptual system; to discover self-esteem; to settle lasting and satisfying relationships with others; to experience, enhance, or establish power; and to encounter meaningful transcendence. McKnight writes of the importance of an advocate in the conversion process, emphasizing that God uses the human relational connection as a key part in each conversion.

> Advocates have one necessary feature: for dynamic communication to take place, and for conversion to follow, the advocate must correlate substantially with the convert and his or her world. That is, the advocate must be able to enter into the potential convert's symbolic universe and show significance. (2002, 84)

What McKnight is referring to relates to what the Bible says concerning the necessity of someone sharing the gospel personally with the convert. "How can they hear without someone preaching to them?" (Rom. 10:14b).

Throughout this process, there is the amazing work of the Spirit of God guiding, cooperating with, and utilizing the involvement of men and women to bring a lost person into God's family. Even though there are common elements, it is unique for each individual and cannot be constrained by a regimented program. It happens mysteriously, by God's grace and love at work in the life of the converted, as well as in the lives of those he uses to bring someone to himself. We have seen many Chinese scholars who are exposed to the gospel and faithful witness for a number of years before they respond. We also have seen some who respond almost immediately upon hearing a clear presentation of the gospel. It is only God who knows the heart of mankind, and we trust him to work in the lives he leads us to minister to. We must "be prepared to give an answer to everyone who asks you to give the reason for the hope that you have." But we also must "do this with gentleness and respect" (1 Peter 3:15).

Eternity on their Hearts

The great news is that God prepares the way, and he includes us as a part of the process; we are not responsible for the whole process. The writer of Ecclesiastes says that God "has set eternity in the human heart." There is an eternal awareness in every heart, regardless of worldview or culture. God has placed within every human being a yearning for something more, a desire for the eternal, and a realization that this life cannot be all that there is. In his book *Mere Christianity*, C.S. Lewis wrote:

> Creatures are not born with desires unless satisfaction for those desires exists. A baby feels hunger: well, there is such a thing as food. A duckling wants to swim: well, there is such a thing as water. Men feel sexual desire: well there is such a thing as sex. If I find in myself a desire which no experience in this world can satisfy, the most probable explanation is that I was made for another world. If none of my earthly pleasures satisfy it, that does not prove that the universe is a fraud. Probably earthly pleasures were never meant to satisfy it, but only to arouse it, to suggest the real thing.

When we encounter a Chinese student or scholar on campus who has just arrived from China, it is encouraging to know that God has already put eternity in the hearts of these students. We can pray, "God lead us to those with whom you want us to share our lives and love," and be assured that he has already been at work. We have heard from many Chinese who have become Christians that they were seeking, or sensed that God was already at work. Here are some statements from Chinese who have come to Christ while in the US:

- "God put that desire inside of me, I completely changed from a 8-year Party member to a Christian, I sometimes don't believe this change could happen to me."
- "I felt that I traveled thousands of miles to America and, on top of that, to come to know Christ. That in itself is quite amazing. I never thought I would become a Christian. But after a process of learning about Christian faith, I came to concur with it more and more. It wasn't anything dramatic that led me to coming to a sudden decision to receive Christ. In fact, the issue of believing in a religion had been on my mind ever since I encountered Christian claims. One day it dawned on me that to believe or not to believe, was all about making a choice, for there was no way to prove it one way or another. I realized that I could choose to believe, and that was also a reasonable choice, logically speaking. I wanted to cross the threshold and to experience it personally."
- "I sought answers in other religions too and felt lonely deep within me and did not find what to trust. But God can listen to my prayer any time. It was God's will that I came to America. Many things happened to me. When I was out in the natural world and strongly felt God's power."
- "Since childhood I have known there must be a supernatural

God. Therefore I believed I should do good deeds. Unfortunately I did not know who he was."

- "I always believed the existence of God, even when I was in China, and I've formed a habit of praying to this God since I was little. That's why when my roommate told me about Jesus and God, I didn't struggle much to believe it. It felt good to finally get to know this God to whom I've been praying."

- "Since childhood I had believed there was a god, and I had always seriously wanted to find him. I had encountered different religions and had some church life in China. However, true change occurred after coming to America. I did a lot of reading of materials which were not available to me in China, and as a result I came to know Jesus as Savior."

There is a desire, put in us by God, to be happy and to enjoy life. We try to find it in many ways. God does give us good things to enjoy, but he also has made us so that we will not find the ultimate happiness and enjoyment in temporary things. Since we have eternity in our hearts, things that are temporary have temporary impact. We yearn for the eternal, and that is only found in him who is eternal. The lack of satisfaction is to drive us to the search for what truly satisfies. St. Augustine said, "Thou has made us for thyself, and our hearts are restless until they learn to rest in Thee."

We find this truth evidenced in the comments of Chinese students and scholars. Many have shared that they came to America to pursue a degree which they hoped would provide them with a better life—and with happiness. We also have heard from many who say that once they reached their goal of a Ph.D. or other degree, there was still something missing. Here are some direct quotes from Chinese scholars:

- "In my past experiences, I had my share of setbacks and sometimes I was not even able to achieve goals that I was sure to be able to reach. But years later, I came to realize that the goals I had were not really the best for me. I felt that God was guiding my way even though I did not know him then and did not have any opportunity to learn about him. It was not until I came to America that I have learned and come to put my trust in him."

- "After about half a year in the US, I decided to become a Christian, primarily for two reasons. First, I had a very sad experience and I wanted to be released. Second, I felt that I needed something to fill my heart instead of my daily schedule. I never had that experience and felt that need when I was in China, but I think that God has been calling for a long time and I finally responded to him."

And God uses the lives of Christians to create a desire in others for what they see:

- "My colleague took me to church. I was deeply attracted by the church life and the peace and joy the Christians had. I was also attracted by how they lived in harmony with one another."

The impact of eternity in their hearts is not just seen in the process of people coming to accept Christ, but it is also a continual part of our lives as we walk with the Lord. We will never be satisfied with things here—God wants us to know him and to love him and to be fulfilled in him. He has made us for himself. We have seen this as people step out in faith to leave jobs, raise support, and move to new areas to be used by God to reach Chinese students and scholars. They are not attracted by a salary, but they are drawn by an eternal purpose, as seen in these examples of many who are becoming a part of God's plan to reach Chinese students and scholars for Christ.

- Peter was a professor of Marxist Philosophy in China before coming to faith and becoming a house church pastor. He came to America to get seminary training to be better equipped as a pastor. Instead, God put it on his heart to share the gospel with those who come to study as future leaders who will soon return to China as influencers.

- Danny had a good job as a project manager, while taking seminary classes online to be prepared to serve God more effectively. He has been volunteering in a large Chinese Church, but felt God's call to serve with COM to reach students who come to America for graduate degrees. He knows that many of these could become multipliers in God's kingdom, if they return to China as followers of Jesus Christ.

- Sunny came from China to the US to continue her Ph.D. studies in Psychology. She said, "I had been a seeker for truth since I was very young. Secular psychology had disappointed me so much by telling me that there was no absolute truth. Therefore, when the Bible told me that Jesus is the way, the life, and the truth, my heart started its journey to follow him." While in America, she became a follower of Jesus and was baptized. She returned to finish her Ph.D. in China. She got involved in a house church and grew in the Lord and in ministry. She came back to the US to study in seminary and received her Master of Divinity with a counseling emphasis and has joined COM to reach Chinese at a key university. There have been challenges in getting her visa, and in raising her support, but she has persevered for the eternal purpose. "I often sense that the Chinese are orphans who do not know their Father, and it is the most joyful thing for me to point them the way back home and lead them into the loving arms of our Heavenly Father!"

The Joy of the Lord in Ministry

A few years ago, our leadership followed a suggested plan to seek God's vision for the ministry. The plan was for me (Glen) as the leader to go away "to the mountain" to pray and seek the Lord. Preceding that event, we met with all of the COM staff, board, and leadership in small vision groups that were moderated by others while I listened and took notes. The groups all answered three questions: 1) What do you believe are the top 2 or 3 gifts God has given to COM; 2) What do you believe are the top 2 or 3 opportunities God has given to COM; and 3) What is your God given dream for COM.

In March I went to the mountain to seek the Lord, taking with me the lists of answers from these groups, a Bible, and a devotional book. I went to a Benedictine monastery in Virginia for two days. During this same time, the COM staff organized a prayer vigil. Getting away, being still before the Lord, and seeking him through prayer was a valuable time in itself. The monastery emphasized silence and solitude, so I had plenty of time to pray and seek the Lord. It also was a time to get some rest. I had a few naps, went to bed early each evening and slept well each night.

When I awoke the first morning, my thoughts were led to reflect and meditate on Psalm 103. "Bless the Lord O my soul, and all that is within me bless his holy name. Bless the Lord O my soul, and forget not his benefits. Who forgives all your sins, and heals all your diseases." I then began to reflect on other passages of Scripture related to the joy of the Lord. "Rejoice in the Lord always, I will say it again, Rejoice!" (Phil. 4:4). "The joy of the Lord is your strength" (Neh. 8:10). "You will go out with joy" (Is. 55:12) — a promise from God through Isaiah to the exiles. I also read the promise in Psalm 37:4, "Delight yourself in the Lord and he will give you the desires of your heart." The joy of the Lord, delighting in the Lord, rejoicing in the Lord, going out with joy — these things resonated in my heart and I began to have a sense that this was a focus that God desired for our ministry. The vision that God showed me is that our outreach to Chinese would be a ministry where the joy of the Lord permeates and guides all that we are and all that we do. It would be a ministry where the joy of the Lord so transforms the lives of Chinese students and scholars that when they return they bring this joy and the aroma of Christ with them.

This raised many questions. How would we do this? What might this look like? What would we do to see this take place? Even perhaps, what are things that rob us of joy and are there ways we can eliminate these? And on the positive, what brings us the joy of the Lord and how can we emphasize this?

My initial thoughts on this were the following:

First, this must begin with our personal, daily walk with the Lord. We know that who we are is a key factor in what we do. So one thing is to intentionally focus on the joy of the Lord. We seek the fruit of joy in the Holy Spirit and ask him to give it and fill us. We consider it all joy when we face various trials (James 1:2) and we are joyful in dealing with each other, with our personal relationships, and relating with Chinese.

Second, in recruitment and training, a joyful heart and spirit will be an essential element emphasized in carrying out the ministry. Certainly, the truth of God's Word and the gospel must be shared, but it should be the joy of knowing the Lord that permeates what we do and how we do it. 1 Peter 1:8 says that "Though you have not seen him, you love him; and even though you do not see him now, you believe in him and are filled with an inexpressible and glorious joy, for you receiving the goal of your faith, the salvation of your souls." God has used this to draw Chinese to himself and will continue to do so more and more. I see joyful Christians being used of God so that many more Chinese will ask us to give an answer for the hope that we have (1 Peter 3:15).

Third, this encourages our partners in ministry—our donors and volunteers. Paul speaks of giving cheerfully (2 Cor. 9:7). When there is joy in living for the Lord and joy in ministry, that joy will encourage and give joy to our supporters so that they give joyfully. And the way we communicate to them is to be full of joy as well.

Fourth, is the picture that Chinese scholars will themselves come to know the joy of the Lord and take that back to China. As we disciple them in Christian growth, we must include an emphasis not only on a knowledge of the Scriptures and the truth of God's Word, but also on what it means to have life in the Spirit and the qualities that result in the joy of the Lord. Life in China (or here in the US) can be difficult, busy and full of pressure with very little joy. A life of joy in the Lord can and will be used by him to influence and draw others.

Jesus said, "I have told you this so that my joy may be in you and that your joy may be complete" (John 15:11). My thoughts come out of experiences that I have already seen—where Chinese students and scholars are deeply touched by joyful lives in Christ and they want this in their lives. One Chinese scholar declared, "The first time I attended the Fellowship, I was shocked by the happiness and joy, the love that people had for God and for each other." This person eventually became a Christian. I believe as we see this more and more, many will believe and take the joy of the Lord back to China and be used mightily of him there, so that many more will believe and live for Jesus.

This testimony of a Chinese scholar who came to study in America illustrates the impact that joy in the life of Christians can have:

> When I was a teenager, I remember reading a poem from the Bible in a friend's notebook. It was about how when I cross the valley of death, God is with me. I was so touched by the poem that I never forgot it. However, I did not believe in God and I don't know that my friend did either. In China, many people, famous scientists, don't believe in God. I believed I could trust them.

> I had a difficult childhood. My mother was very tough and didn't understand us. I lost my father when I was very young. At college I felt very free, free from my mother. I had some love affairs, but in my heart I was not happy. I didn't like myself. I thought no one really loved me. When I got married I didn't have a good understanding of myself. In the next ten years, I had so much pressure from my family and my work. I felt like my husband couldn't satisfy me. We had many troubles. I was so disappointed in my life. Sometimes I didn't even want to live.

> When I came with my son to study in the US, I worried about how to take care of him by myself. One of my friends told me that if I needed help I could go to a church. So, after a few days I asked someone to recommend a church to me.

I called the pastor's wife. She was kind and welcoming. When I went to church, I was impressed. Many people there had Ph.Ds. and were intellectuals and professors, yet they prayed and sang. It was hard to believe. With my background in atheism, it was difficult to consider giving up all that I knew to trust Jesus. But I remembered the poem, and I asked where I could find it. Someone said it was from Psalm 23.

I began to take part in their fellowship and Bible study. At first I wanted to argue. I argued that Christianity was not respectful of women. I was looking for reasons not to believe in Jesus.

I tried to learn more about Christianity. I borrowed books from the church and read online testimonies. I began to think that perhaps I should believe in God. I was often depressed, and I thought that this might be a way out. I finally decided to accept Jesus as my Savior, but I didn't want to be baptized. From then on I began to read the Bible every day. I found some peace but that peace was not stable. I still struggled with depression.

I met with a strong Christian lady and told her about my depression. As she talked with me, I realized I should be baptized. I could not have consistent peace while holding back something for myself. I talked with the pastor, and he said I must decide. I finally took the next step to go into the water. I surrendered to Jesus.

I am thankful that God found me. For a long time I was lost. I worked hard and studied hard. I felt responsibility for myself and my son. I tried to find myself in entertainment, shopping and the Internet. I went from one thing to the next. But there was no foundation for happiness or peace. I thought I had the right to enjoy life. I was searching for something to fill the gap in my heart. Now those things are not necessary for me. I have a deep foundation for peace and joy. I can rest in his big and deep ocean of love.

When I think back to before I arrived here, I see that the Lord had been leading me for a long time and that he prepared me to know him. Some people ask why I became a Christian so fast, but I believe that God had been preparing me. I had a heart for truth, but I couldn't find truth in my country. Even though I didn't know what truth was, I kept thinking there must be truth. Whenever I met a Christian, Chinese or American, I would ask the same question, "When you became a Christian, what did you get?" They all answered "peace and joy." I had no peace and joy. That moved me because Chinese people don't have peace and joy.

This summer my daughter, who is fifteen, flew to America all by herself. I told God that I wanted to introduce her to Jesus. I didn't expect my daughter to become a Christian right then, but I thought maybe God would plant a seed in her heart. I didn't force her to become a Christian. I just took her to church and read the Bible to her. She admired the good behavior in Christians, and she saw the change in me. So she was baptized the same day as I was. I am so thankful! Now my husband is reading the Bible, and I think that someday he will be a Christian and we will be a Christian family.

Part Three

Practical Tips, Insights, Approach, Perspectives

Chapter 9

Keys to Cross-cultural Communication with Chinese Intellectuals

A typical communication process starts with the sender having an intent to communicate and ends with the feedback from the receiver. This process consists of the following steps:

1. The sender conceptualizing his intended idea. This is the initial planning stage where the sender mentally develops his idea and decides what to communicate.

2. Encoding his idea. The sender turns his conceptual idea into a format that is to be conveyed to the receiver.

3. Transmitting the message through a medium. The sender formulates a message that can be transmitted to the receiver through a medium such as oral, textual or simply nonverbal such as winking or gesturing.

4. Decoding. The receiver interacts with the message through analysis and interpretation in order to understand the sender's intent as embodied in the message.

5. The communication is successful if the receiver understands

the message as intended by the sender. This is only possible if both the sender and the receiver are competent communicators who follow the same rules of the language and understand the denotation and connotation of the words (or nonverbal cues) used in the process.

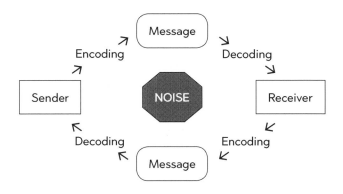

The Communications Process

The feedback process (the bottom half of the chart) includes the same components, except that the receiver becomes the sender, and the sender, the receiver.

If we apply the process to a cross-cultural communication setting between an English-speaking American and a Chinese student, we immediately can see the challenges that need to be overcome. A Chinese student is likely not a competent communicator in English, despite the great efforts they have spent acquiring English as a second language; nor is an American a competent communicator in Chinese. The good news is that we do not need to be perfect, but we do need to strive to be good communicators. Also, we need to keep in mind that we are not alone in this process, because the Holy Spirit promises to be with us and work through us despite our deficiency.

Even though we have little control over the receiver's decoding of our message, we can verify how our message has been received by checking on the feedback from the receiver. If the feedback confirms our intent, then our communication has been successful. If not, then there has been a breakdown or distortion. For example, if you invite a Chinese friend to your home for dinner, and he hesitates initially but later says yes, you need to verify that his yes really means yes. You may want to get more feedback from him by asking some follow-up questions such as what time he is planning to come and if he needs a ride. You may also want to pay attention to see if he is engaged in talking with you about the details. If he seems to be disengaged regarding the details, it is highly likely that his yes does not mean he is planning on coming to dinner. He may respond as a typical Chinese who has difficulty saying no, especially to a kind invitation. If that is the case, don't rush to put your turkey in the oven for dinner.

Throughout the communication process, both in the transmission and feedback phases, we need to be aware of "noise" and do our best to minimize it wherever possible. Noise is not necessarily anything audible. It refers to any disruption that interferes with or distorts the sender's intent in the transmission phase from the sender to the receiver or in the feedback phase. Noise can occur in any stage of the communication process, but it often occurs during encoding and decoding. These two areas are the most prone to distortions due to our language and cultural backgrounds. For example, when you says "God loves the world" to a Chinese who is not familiar to the Christian world views, "God" is likely an abstract concept, or merely as someone powerful. He likely associates your "God" with "one of the gods out there." In Chinese folk religions, gods may reside anywhere. There are river gods, kitchen gods, tree gods, or gods in the sea. Also in Buddhism, there are many gods with powers in specific spheres, and people choose which god to pray to depending on their needs. In cross-cultural communication, we have to explain the terms we use or even paraphrase them in order to achieve success in communication.

In communication with Chinese, noise may come from a wide variety of areas—cultural background, theological views (Chinese polytheistic culture), personal experiences (past encounters with Christians using aggressive methods of evangelism), spiritual factors (the Devil is busy at work), environmental factors (noisy children in the background), physiological issues (physical tiredness), language competence (poor command of English), tone, connotations, non-verbal cues, and attitude.

Something is always lost in the communication process. According to research, it has been estimated that even in the best scenarios, communication is only eighty percent effective! So be aware that the next time you say "I love you" to your spouse, your love message will likely be stronger or weaker than you originally intended after it is decoded. This is even more true with cross-cultural communication.

Chapter 10

Security Concerns

There tends to be two extremes with regards to security issues. Some people seem to be paranoid, as if the Chinese government is keeping track of every Chinese student who attends church activities or Bible study groups. On the other hand, there are those who do not appear to have any security awareness at all and openly publicize pictures of Chinese students, including their real names.

Security is a concern because of the Chinese government's attitude toward Christianity and toward Christians. It is important to be informed of how Beijing views Christianity so that we may approach this issue appropriately. The view of many Americans still reflects an understanding of China from the Mao era, while the reality is that China has undergone profound changes. Even the Chinese government's view and approach to Christianity has changed significantly. During the Mao era, the government was very simplistic and tried to eradicate all religions, Christianity in particular. However, the present government has become more sophisticated and has come to realize that religions, including Christianity, are a reality that even an atheistic country like China may need to live with for a long time. One telling example is that in 2016, 150 million copies of the Bible were printed in

China. The world's largest Bible printing company is based in China: Amity Printing Company, which is a joint venture between the Amity Foundation, a Chinese charity, and the United Bible Societies.

However, it is not Beijing's intent to give genuine freedom to Christians. More personal freedom and choice in China is not a gracious gift from the communist government; rather, it has come about as a part of the dynamic changes in China resulting from globalization, which accelerated after China joined the World Trade Organization in 2001. The Beijing government has merely shifted from the Mao era goal of eradicating religions to a stance of managing and controlling religion. This change, however, marks a significant difference.

Persecution of Christians in China still exists in varying degrees. It continues to be important for the international community to speak out for the voiceless and the persecuted. There are real cases of persecution, though many of them have been exaggerated, leaving readers with a less than truthful impression of the current reality in China.

What is usually not reported, unfortunately, is the less sensational but widespread discrimination against Christians throughout the country. This is especially true for Christians working in the government sector — in universities, research institutes and government agencies. In these contexts, Christians are under the pressure to hide their religious identities. If they are known to be Christian, they will be the last ones to be promoted in their professional career. Such pressure can come and go depending on where it stands on Beijing's priority list. Ironically, such persecution and discrimination may in reality reflect the government's concern and desperation in trying to contain and control the growing Christian church in China.

Even though the Chinese government is ideologically bankrupt, many people still choose to join the Communist Party in order to gain the benefits associated with Party membership. One of the demands of being a Party member is to be an atheist and not believe in any religion or join any religious organization. Under President Xi Jinping, Beijing is concerned about many Party members becoming Christians. Party members are now required to reaffirm their atheist belief. Those who have chosen to be affiliated with any religion are purged from the Party. However, the issue at stake is not so much about belief, as it is about loyalty and commitment. The Beijing government is pressuring Party members to answer this question: "Is your first loyalty to the Communist Party, or to Jesus or any other gods or religions?" This is at the heart of the government efforts.

Many visiting scholars and graduate students are members of the Communist Party, although they are instructed not to reveal that during the US visa application process. Fewer undergraduates are Party members. The same pressure from the atheist Beijing government will be applied to visiting scholars and students when they return to China. This is especially so for those who are Party members. Upon their return, they will be asked if they are affiliated with or if they have joined any religious organizations during their study overseas.

How is affiliation or membership in an organization defined? Most definitely, if a Chinese is baptized, the government will consider him or her as having affiliated or joined the Christian religion. This is a line in the sand for the Chinese.

It is important for Christian workers to be aware of this line because baptism has a lot to do with the security concerns. Next to baptism, any public confession of faith will likely be considered as affiliation with or membership in a religious group. In light of the factors above, it is important that we Christian workers respect the need for privacy and security.

On the other hand, we do not need to be paranoid. It is normally not a security concern for the average Chinese student and scholar, including Party members, to attend Christian activities such as Sunday services, Bible studies, retreats and conferences, or to have interaction with Christians individually. These activities are likely viewed as part of living in a Western society. They do not constitute any formal affiliation with or membership in any religious group. A visiting scholar with an official status in China will not likely publicly participate in religious activities, though he or she may be willing to interact with Christians privately. Further, as China's private sector grows, more and more people are working in the private sector where there is little or no discrimination against Christians. For this reason, students or scholars from the private sector will likely not have security concerns. However, there are always exceptions.

For Christian workers, proper caution and common sense should be applied when publicizing any ministry newsletter involving work among Chinese. The key question to ask is: "If our newsletter, article or email ends up in the hands of the Chinese authority, will any of our Chinese contacts be implicated?" If the answer is yes, then we should not publicize it. In our age of the internet and cell phones, all it takes is a click for our newsletter to be forwarded to the Chinese embassy or all the way to China. Unless you receive specific permission from your Christian friends, it is not advisable to publish a picture of a Chinese person getting baptized along with personal information that can be traced—such as name, school, location, etc.

A Chinese student's interaction with Christians can fall into a spectrum from casual to serious. On the more casual end of the spectrum are activities such as meeting with Christian friends, picnics, trips, church potlucks, Christmas concerts, and occasional Sunday services.

On the more serious end are activities such as regularly attending Sunday worship, giving open testimonies, getting baptized, receiving seminary training, and giving public testimony through the media.

Chapter 11

Finding Open Doors Through Felt Needs

It is often said that the Chinese tend to be practical and do not like to spend time dealing with what they see as abstract or irrelevant. They tend to focus on the here and now. While this type of mindset has its weaknesses, it does give Christians an open door to build a relationship through meeting felt needs. Felt needs are the needs they can feel, not the needs we think they should feel. The Chinese usually do not feel they have spiritual needs as we Christians understand. They tend to feel their spiritual needs much later in their interaction with Christians.

Their felt needs may change depending on their life's circumstances. Some needs are one time or occasional while other needs are ongoing. Their felt needs also differ from person to person. An undergraduate student from an affluent family background may want to buy a new car as soon as he arrives in the US and may not appreciate used furniture at all. In contrast, a visiting scholar with a limited budget will appreciate used furniture and may just want to buy a used car to drive for a year or two. Again, stereotyping will not work here.

But in general, we list here some felt needs:

When they have just arrived in America the first time, their felt needs may include:

- Airport pickups
- Help with registration at school
- Locating temporary housing
- Opening a checking account
- Getting a social security number (for ID purposes)
- Getting rides for shopping and errands
- Language help
- Making new friends
- Car purchase
- Used furniture

Ongoing or occasional felt needs:

- Language help
- Friendship
- Host families
- Learning to drive and get a license
- Sense of a community
- Rides (airport, doctor, appointments, etc.)
- Baby sitting
- Help with moving (Trucks, vans, packing)
- Marital issues (communication, help with conflict resolution)
- Understanding American culture, customs, holidays, sports
- Cultural tips: what to say or do on what occasion?
- Raising children
- Help with life situations (car accidents, rental leases, disputes, changing advisors, interacting with medical personnel, etc.)

- Trips out of town
- Getting advice and referrals (finding doctors, auto mechanics)
- Preparing for an interview (how to dress, résumé, etc.)

Chapter 12

How to Address Typical Questions

Due to their upbringing in a different cultural and atheistic background, Chinese students and scholars tend to look at Christianity from a different angle. In addition, they tend to be very well-educated with a strong background in science. If you do not speak Chinese, they will likely be using English as a second language to discuss with Christian workers about Christian faith. These combined factors present a challenge for Christians.

There are no standard answers that can be cut and pasted to questions typically raised by Chinese. That would be wishful thinking. An answer well received by one Chinese may not go as well with another. Students with a science background think very differently from those with a humanities background. People with different past experiences respond to Christian views very differently. People in different age groups also show varying levels of spiritual interest and think differently.

Despite the personal differences, some approaches seem to be effective and appropriate based on my 25 years of ministry to the Chinese, and I (Daniel) would like to recommend them here:

1. **Recognize the spiritual dimension of our outreach.** We need to be consciously aware that unless the Lord builds the house, the laborers labor in vain. We need to always rely on prayer and count on the work of the Holy Spirit. This is not just an evangelically correct statement to make. I truly believe it makes a difference. It takes spiritual power, not our articulation, to break a spiritual stronghold.

2. **Focus on the common ground shared by all Christians.** If a Chinese student is at the initial stage of spiritual interest, discussion topics should focus on basic Christian teachings shared by all Christians without getting into unique perspectives held dearly only by a particular Christian group. It can be very confusing for the Chinese to discuss these unique perspectives. It is good to know the strengths and limitations of your own theological framework. If you are a strong Calvinist, your answers to questions raised by the Chinese could be very different from the answers given by a free-will Baptist. It is helpful to clarify that your answer is from your own particular theological vantage point and may not be shared by all other Christians. It demonstrates a breadth in Christian faith and the uniqueness we have of unity within our diversity. This can help our friends realize that becoming a Christian leads to a personal change, and not human conformity. That helps keep us humble, doesn't it? Whenever possible, it seems best to focus on the common positions held by all Christians.

3. **Be sensitive to the fact that your Chinese friend is using English as a second language.** That means we need to use

simple English; we need to define and explain our theological terms and use examples and analogies to help them understand; we also need to listen to their feedback to verify they really understand what we say.

4. **Be willing to say we don't have a good answer.** We don't really lose anything by this simple acknowledgement. Instead, we gain their respect by our honesty and humility. In fact, I have seen more damage done by Christians who really did not have the right answer but responded with an inappropriate answer that turned people off. Instead, we can always say we'll be glad to do some research and see if we can find an answer later. Or we can throw the ball back to him and say: "That's a great question. Honestly, I don't have a good answer. Do you?"

Here is a list of questions Chinese students and scholars tend to have. They may or may not ask you these directly. You may not have the perfect answers for all the questions, but it is good to be as prepared as we can. At least, we want to be aware of their questions.

1. Is America a Christian nation? If yes, how come there are still so many problems in America?
2. Why did the Western Christian nations invade China, burn our Summer Palace and commit atrocities against the Chinese people during the Opium War in the 19th century?
3. Why are there so many churches bearing different names? Are they all the same or different?
4. What's the differences between Christians, Catholics, Mormons and Jehovah Witnesses? Do they believe in the same

God? If they do, how come they do not seem to get along with one another?

5. Is the Christian faith compatible with science?

6. How can you prove to me that miracles did happen as recorded in the Bible?

7. What are arguments or evidences to support the view that God exists?

8. How do Christians view evolution?

9. Do Christians seriously believe in creationism?

10. How can I be a good scientist and a good Christian at the same time?

11. If Christianity is not anti-science, why is it that the academic community seems to be biased against Christians?

12. Is the Bible truly God's inspiration?

13. There are so many fantastic miracle claims in the Bible, why should I believe in them?

14. Why was God so cruel in the Old Testament?

15. Does the Old Testament, written by Jews, reflect a Jewish racial superiority and bias against non-Jewish people?

16. Why did God choose the Jews, but not the Chinese, as his people?

17. Is Christianity a kind of cultural imperialism in the hands of Western governments?

18. Why doesn't the Bible say anything about China or the Chinese people, with such a long history as a civilization?

19. Why did God have Jesus born in the land of the Jews? If Jesus had been Chinese, I would have believed in him.

20. If salvation is only found in Jesus, how about my grandparents and those many generations before Christ who never had a

chance to hear the name Jesus and to put their trust in him?

21. If God wants to forgive people, why didn't he just do it without having Jesus suffer on the cross?

22. If someone did evil all his life and became a Christian just before he died and he ended up in heaven, and another person did good deeds all his life but never believed in Jesus and he ended up in hell—wouldn't that make God unfair?

23. If God has a son as the Bible says, how can the son be of the equal status as the concept of Trinity seems to suggest?

24. If I were to become a Christian, wouldn't that create a disharmony in my family because my spouse and parents do not share the same belief?

25. If I return to China as a Christian, would I face persecution and discrimination?

26. Christians need to go to church every Sunday and donate to the church. I don't think I'm ready for that. Can I just be a Christian at heart?

27. Can I just be a good Christian without getting baptized?

Chapter 13

Is Christianity Anti-Science
or Pro-Truth?

Among the Chinese, there is a strong desire to want to know and follow truth in all spheres of life. In some ways, truth is particularly important because of what they have experienced in China's modern history. The Chinese once believed in communism's claims of truth, but they are now disillusioned. The Chinese Communists have always proclaimed that truth is found in the teachings of Marxism and socialism. However, this generation of Chinese have witnessed the collapse of the communist empire in the former Soviet Union, the corruption of Chinese government officials who preach truths but live contrary to their truth claims, and the radical switch in China from a top-down socialist controlled economy to a market economy. The Chinese are now asking, "Where then can we find truth?"

It has been observed that conservative Christian evangelicals tend to focus on the theme of personal salvation. Important as it is, most non-Christian Chinese tend to see salvation as somewhat remote and irrelevant, at least in their initial contact with Christians. Due to Chinese mainstream propaganda, many Chinese think that religions, including Christianity, are superstitious and anti-science. Chinese school textbooks make fun of the church in the medieval period because of its firm opposition to the heliocentric view of the earth going around the sun (advocated by contemporary early modern astronomers like Copernicus and Galileo), due to a literal interpretation of the Bible.

How Christians view science and express the Bible's teaching on science or the universe will have a significant impact on how the educated Chinese view Christianity. This is especially true for the Chinese studying on US campuses, since most of them deal with science academically. A Chinese would think, if the Bible is God's revelation as Christians proclaim, then it should be truthful. Even if the Bible was not written as a science textbook, at least it should not be anti-science.

Christian workers need to properly form their view on science. Is it anti-science or pro-truth? We know true science should agree with reality and false science does not. However, we need to be very cautious in declaring that the Bible teaches one particular scientific theory. Instead, we need to keep in mind that science and its theories are always progressing and never perfect. It is appropriate and harmless to share our opinion regarding a certain theory, but we should never sound as if we are God's spokesmen on certain theories. In this area, a healthy dose of humility is needed, for it could prevent us from creating obstacles for our Chinese friends who are trying to understand our faith.

One such example is the change of viewpoint by many Christians on the big-bang theory. When the theory was first introduced, many evangelical Christians viewed it with disdain and suspected it to be a new theory advocating the same old atheism. But later, as more scientific evidence seems to support the theory, more Christians have embraced it and some Christian speakers equate the moment of the big-bang explosion to the moment of God's creation, subtly suggesting that the Genesis account of creation has been verified by modern science.

The Chinese believe that truth should be in harmony with true science and questions about truth are important in the conversion process. It is therefore highly important that Christian workers be trained to be able to articulate the Christian message in a way that respects and upholds all truth — spiritual, moral, historical and scientific. It is unwise for Christians to baptize a scientific theory. Given time, a new and better theory will likely emerge to replace it.

It would be more helpful for Christians to simply state that the Bible teaches God is the creator of all, without speculating how he did it. That way we do not run the risk of saying too much, having to defend too much, and being viewed as anti-science. As the writer of Hebrews declares, "By faith we understand that the universe was formed at God's command" (Heb. 11:3).

Chapter 14

Dos and Don'ts in Ministry to Chinese

The following are some practical tips that might help you relate to the Chinese. These are general tips, even though you will likely meet some Chinese to whom the following dos and don'ts do not perfectly apply. As individuals, especially if we live in the West, we feel we have rights and are entitled to our own opinions and freedom of speech. But in ministry settings it seems wise not to emphasize our own opinions for the good of others. We feel that this is Christian love and discipline in action. The Bible says, "...not everything is beneficial" (1 Cor. 6:12). On the other hand, the assumptions and opinions of the Chinese, or anyone else's, are not necessarily right either. It seems best to show respect and leave room for the differences while putting a higher priority on topics that are more important and significant.

Dos...

- **Do use an inductive approach in communicating biblical truths, if possible.** An inductive approach in ministry is to start a conversation on a common ground with your Chinese friends and lead the conversion to a biblical truth. For example, you could start by talking about the beauty of nature, discuss with them, and conclude it with your biblical perspective that a loving, powerful creator, rather than a random chance, must be behind it all. Your Chinese friend will likely think that your conclusion makes logical sense.

In contrast, a deductive approach starts from the biblical supposition that God is the creator. This is the reason why we see the beauty and design in creation. Your Chinese friend is not going to say "amen" to that, since he does not believe in the biblical assumption to start with. Most likely he will keep quiet and be polite rather than voice a different opinion.

An inductive approach is more effective because it starts with common ground rather than a different viewpoint. It doesn't require a Christian assumption that a non-Christian does not have. This approach requires more skill and preparation.

- **Do provide Christian hospitality.** Many Chinese scholars may have never been invited to an American home. They are usually very appreciative and curious about what American homes are like and how American family members interact with each other. They are also curious about homemade American food. Christians who lovingly open their homes to Chinese tend to leave them with a lasting impression. The Chinese can do all the sightseeing they want in America, but unless invited, they will never get to visit an American family at home. It's a wonderful experience that a Chinese tourist will never get. It is almost always a positive spiritual experience when they visit a Christian family in their home.

- **Do offer practical help to them especially when they first arrive in America.** Chinese are very practical people. Hence, they greatly appreciate acts of service and kindness. Such acts speak ever more powerfully when they come from non-Chinese because they normally already expect other Chinese will help them due to their cultural affinity. But when non-Chinese such as Americans take the initiatives to offer help, they are pleasantly surprised. Since they need more help when they first arrive, this is the best time to establish a relationship with them. Once they have settled down, their "felt needs" are met and they have made friends, it is harder to reach them.

- **Do try to maintain a long-term relationship despite lack of visible progress.** Your long-term friendship will allow you to continue to be a godly influence in your Chinese friend's life. Over the years, we have seen many Chinese scholars come to Christ and become mature Christian leaders within their churches and communities. Some of them come to Bible studies as students but do not accept the Lord until later in life. As sowers of the gospel seeds, we may not see immediate spiritual results. However, through maintaining our relationships with the Chinese scholars, we can continue to be used by God to positively influence their lives.

- **Do be patient with your Chinese friends.** Pray for them and share with them the love of God through words and deeds.

Allow them time to ask questions. When they start to ask meaningful spiritual questions, this is a sign they are seriously seeking. Some stay at this seeking stage for a few months and others for much longer before they truly commit themselves to Christ. As Christians, we are eager to share the Gospel, but we need to be patient when it comes to reaching out to the Chinese. If our approach is too aggressive, the Chinese, who are brought up as atheists, may feel pressured and uncomfortable because they are not ready to take a leap of faith. At the same time, they may find it difficult to say no or to disagree. Keep in mind that the Chinese are generally polite, and that silence does not mean agreement. It usually takes longer for them to be convinced of Christian beliefs such as the existence of the Creator God, the inspiration of the Bible, the deity of Christ, and salvation through faith in Christ.

- **Do keep a healthy distance between your God and your government or political views.** In cross-cultural ministry, it is important that we see our identity first and foremost as a child of God. All other identities are secondary (such as American, Chinese, Texan, Californian, Republican, Democrat, NRA member, Rush Limbaugh follower, liberal, conservative, NPR supporter, members of a country club or 700 Club). We need to be careful not to leave the wrong impression with our Chinese friends that to be a Christian means they need to hold the same opinions we do. Since we have a higher allegiance to the God above, we are free to critique all earthly things—including how our countrymen live their lives and how our government runs our country or our foreign policies.

Don'ts...

- **Don't pressure the Chinese to accept Jesus.** Some Chinese have had very negative encounters with aggressive Christians pressuring them to pray to receive the Lord. In some extreme cases, Christians even threatened not to leave the apartment where the Chinese lived until they prayed to receive Christ. Unfortunately, some Chinese did pray the sinner's prayer—not to receive Christ but to get rid of the Christians. As you can imagine, such news spreads through the local Chinese community. What a reputation the Christians gained! Other Chinese scholars got invited to Christian homes for dinner and felt pressured to pray to receive Christ. So, they did, but more as a way to pay back their host for their hospitality than to truly commit their lives to Christ. We believe the Chinese should be given genuine freedom in a no pressure environment to respond to the gospel invitation. Any pressure or sales tactics will not lead to a genuine conversion in the heart and is not God-honoring.

- **Don't assume you need to run the whole nine yards for God.** A Chinese usually takes a longer faith journey before finally coming to know Christ. Almost always, God uses different people at different time and location to help him progress spiritually. Rarely does God use just one person to lead someone to Christ from beginning to end. If that is the case, it means we all need to be faithful in doing our "part" in the faith journey of our Chinese friend. Our part could be helping him come to believe that there must be a God out there, or accept the Bible as God's inspiration, or pray to receive Christ as his Lord and Savior. Of course, the last leg of the journey is the most exciting and makes a great report. But in a sense, each step along the journey is just as important as the last step of faith because it requires the same faithful ministry of every Christian.

On the other hand, we do not need to feel discouraged if our Chinese friend has not yet come to know Christ. Your friend will most likely be closer to knowing God than before he met you because of your witness. In a real sense, you have been faithful and have already made a difference in his life.

- **Don't initiate discussion about sensitive geopolitical issues.** This is especially true if your relationship with your Chinese friend is not strong enough to withstand the tension and emotions that might arise from discussing such controversial topics as disputes over islands in South China Sea, sovereignty disputes with Japan over islands in East China Sea, the Taiwan issue, abortion in China, or the One China policy.

- **Don't be offended if Chinese ask personal questions.** Chinese are very curious about America and how Americans live, and the Chinese sense of privacy is not as strong as it is for Americans. Do not be offended if they ask you how much your house is worth. This question is most likely in their minds and might come up when they visit your home. When asked this question, I tend to answer by telling them the range of the house values in my neighborhood. This is often enough to satisfy their curiosity. One time my colleague was asked by his Chinese friend how much he made. He smiled and answered: "Not very much."

- **Don't stereotype.** None of us would do this intentionally, but we might appear to be doing just this unintentionally. China has been undergoing dramatic changes and it is a country with many contradictions and contrasts. Chinese studying in America come from diverse backgrounds. Most are brought up as atheists, but some are Buddhists, Muslims and even Christians. While many Chinese scholars and students are more affluent than those who came a decade ago, some may come from poorer families in China. It is better to have them tell their background and life stories rather than for us to voice our naive assumptions in the beginning.

- **Don't criticize the Chinese government.** Most Chinese will not voice that their government is great, but many may feel American criticism of China as a personal loss of face. These same students may be very critical of their government when talking with their Chinese friends, but the dynamics change when Americans are the ones criticizing the Chinese government. They may feel the need to defend their own government. As China's influence grows with its expanding economy, nationalism has been on the rise. More and more Chinese are proud of being Chinese and proud of China rising as a stronger nation. Many Chinese are seeing their personal well-being now directly connected with China as a nation.

Chapter 15

Biblical Perspectives on Ministry to Chinese

The Bible has many wonderful teachings about how to relate to people. They are also very relevant to ministry to the Chinese. The following select passages are not only great for meditation but they can serve as principles to follow for our ministry.

Motivated by love

Love is patient, love is kind. It does not envy, it does not boast, it is not proud. It does not dishonor others, it is not self-seeking, it is not easily angered, it keeps no record of wrongs. Love does not delight in evil but rejoices with the truth. It always protects, always trusts, always hopes, always perseveres. (1 Cor. 13:4-7)

This love passage perfectly spells out the key principle for our ministry to the Chinese — the principle of love. Without love, our ministry would be in vain — a total waste of our time and energy. Human motivation is always complex and mysterious. We may do the same thing outwardly but have a different motivation inwardly. The Bible says: "The heart is deceitful above all things and beyond cure. Who can understand it?" (Jer. 17:9). In our ministry, we are not always motivated by love alone. Sometimes, our motivation may be less than completely pure because as fallen human beings we are still less than perfect. In my ministry, I was greatly inspired by these words by Mother Teresa: "Not all of us can do great things. But we can do small things with great love." May God continue to do his work of transformation within us that we may reflect more of him and less of us.

Being faithful where God puts us

> *What, after all, is Apollos? And what is Paul? Only servants, through whom you came to believe—as the Lord has assigned to each his task. I planted the seed, Apollos watered it, but God has been making it grow. So, neither the one who plants nor the one who waters is anything, but only God, who makes things grow. The one who plants and the one who waters have one purpose, and they will each be rewarded according to their own labor. For we are co-workers in God's service...* (1 Cor. 3:5-9)

Everything happens for a reason. God's good purpose is at work when we meet Chinese students, wherever they are in their faith journey. We are God's gift to them at their particular stage of the journey. We could be a Paul who plants the seed, or an Apollos who waters the seed. We want to be faithful with the window of opportunity God has given us. We may not be the ones to lead them all the way to faith in Christ. Our calling is to be faithful and help them get closer to knowing God, one step at a time. Even if they never reach the point of placing their faith in Christ during their lifetime, we would still be glad that we loved them and that we were faithful with the opportunities we were given. No act of kindness, no matter how small, is ever wasted. During his ministry on earth, Jesus fed and healed many people, though most of them never came to trust in Him. As Thomas Merton, a Catholic monk, puts it well: "Love seeks one thing only: the good of the one loved. It leaves all the other secondary effects to take care of themselves. Love, therefore, is its own reward." May we likewise be rewarded.

Leave the results to God

> *A farmer went out to sow his seed. As he was scattering the seed, some fell along the path; it was trampled on, and the birds ate it up. Some fell on rocky ground, and when it came up, the plants withered because they had no moisture. Other seed fell among thorns, which grew up with it and choked the plants. Still other seed fell on good soil. It came up and yielded a crop, a hundred times more than was sown. (Luke 8:5-8)*

As we minister to people, we do not know who will receive Christ. Or from a Calvinist viewpoint, we do not know who is predestined. Our job is to do our part faithfully—sowing the seed in this parable. After that, we leave the results to God. This does not mean we do not need to evaluate and seek improvement, but it does mean that the visible results are not necessarily a good indicator of our faithfulness. Jesus would have been a fantastic failure if he was judged by how many people were following him at the end of his earthly ministry. In eternity I believe we will be held accountable for our faithfulness in the opportunities we were given, rather than how many people we have brought to heaven. In ministry to the Chinese, we must not be discouraged when we do not see as much fruit as we would like. When there is much fruit, it is a reminder that God has been at work. In all things, we give him the glory.

Serve as if Jesus was in need

When the Son of Man comes in his glory, and all the angels with him, he will sit on his glorious throne. All the nations will be gathered before him, and he will separate the people one from another as a shepherd separates the sheep from the goats. He will put the sheep on his right and the goats on his left. Then the King will say to those on his right, 'Come, you who are blessed by my Father; take your inheritance, the kingdom prepared for you since the creation of the world. For I was hungry and you gave me something to eat, I was thirsty and you gave me something to drink, I was a stranger and you invited me in, I needed clothes and you clothed me, I was sick and you looked after me, I was in prison and you came to visit me.' Then the righteous will answer him, 'Lord, when did we see you hungry and feed you, or thirsty and give you something to drink? When did we see you a stranger and invite you in, or needing clothes and clothe you? When did we see you sick or in prison and go to visit you?' The King will reply, 'Truly I tell you, whatever you did for one of the least of these brothers and sisters of mine, you did for me.' (Matt. 25:40-45)

What a reminder this is to be aware of and serve those around us—the needy person we serve could be none other than our Lord! I remember one time I met an elderly couple in their late 60s who came to the US to visit with their son and babysit their grandson. Their son was in a Ph.D. program in a state university along the East Coast. A few months after their arrival, the elderly couple began to look very distressed. Later we began to hear stories that they were mistreated and harassed at home; some abuse seemed to have also taken place. The elderly man had to sleep on the floor of the apartment. He began to develop high blood pressure and nervousness. In desperation, they sought help. Their Chinese neighbor saw their misery and helped them book air tickets for a flight back to China. They came and literally begged me to give them a ride to the airport for their escape. When the day to leave came, I met them at the parking lot of the apartment. They hurriedly got into my car without their son's notice. They gave a sigh of relief as I sped off onto the highway. Then they began to weep. They did not dare to inform their son until a few minutes before boarding their flight at the airport.

That was the first time I served such needy and desperate people. It was stressful and I felt sad for the elderly couple. The only consolation I had was that what I did for them, I did for my Lord. The Chinese have come to America far away from home and families. They run into different kinds of needy situations. Their needs become our opportunities to serve, build relationships, and share God's love. By serving them, we serve our Lord.

Avoid arguments and controversies

> *Don't have anything to do with foolish and stupid arguments, because you know they produce quarrels. And the Lord's servant must not be quarrelsome but must be kind to everyone, able to teach, not resentful. (2 Tim. 2:23-24)*

It is important to keep in mind our mission in ministry is to share the love of Christ. Everything else should be secondary. While we may be passionate about particular theological positions, political topics or geopolitical issues, it is important that we keep these in check so that our personal viewpoints may not negatively affect our missions. It is not our mission to convert the Chinese to our church sub-culture or political persuasions. However, it is normal in any relationship to share ideas and exchange our view points. One of the risks is that we may become too passionate or emotional during a discussion, and feelings and relationships can be damaged. There is also the risk that we might spend more time on controversial issues than focusing on our primary mission of sharing God's love. We need to discipline ourselves and remain focused on our mission.

Chapter 16

Chinese and Americans Working Together

At COM we have been blessed to have moved from a fully Caucasian American staff to twenty percent being native-born Chinese. Some of these staff came to America as students and scholars and met Christ. The cultural differences among staff can be a challenge, but also a strength as we reach out to Mainland Chinese students and scholars. Caucasian American staff seem to have an advantage over Chinese in initial connections with Chinese scholars coming to study in America. This relates to the Chinese concept of *guanxi*. Jackson Wu cites Andrew Kipnis, Anthropology Professor at Australian National University, who explains that *guanxi* involves reciprocity and human feelings, entails social and material obligations, and points to the web of in-group relationships within one's daily life. Because of this, incoming Chinese are suspicious of Chinese in America reaching out to help them. They anticipate that there will be a time for paying back. This does not appear to be an expectation as they relate to Americans. There is also the "welcoming to our country" factor that demonstrates the power of the biblical encouragement of hospitality to the stranger.

The desire to experience American culture creates an openness to Americans willing to help with adjustment and understanding in this new culture. There is also the thought of America being a Christian country, and a perspective that America's success is associated with its Christian heritage. Fenggang Yang points out that in the Chinese scholar's mind Christianity is linked to "progressive, liberating, modern, and universal" concepts. In light of this, American missionaries have an advantage in reaching out to Chinese intellectuals when they first arrive. The friendship they provide and the loving caring relationships are an important aspect attracting Chinese to Christ. But Americans are also limited because of language and cultural understanding. When it comes to deeper understanding and discussions, particularly in fully understanding faith and for follow up and discipleship, Chinese are most effective.

When the two cultures work together, effectiveness increases, especially when there is cooperation and appreciation for each other's strengths. The point made by Lianne Roembke concerning advantages and challenges in multi-cultural teams apply here. Advantages include: the unity of Christians across cultures as a testimony to the power of the gospel, a greater network of resources, and providing deeper cross-cultural understanding. There are also challenges, including misunderstandings, team members feeling cultural differences are too great to overcome, and the willingness to commit to be a team.

Even though team unity can be positive in demonstrating the gospel, team disunity can be detrimental and discourage belief. As the research data shows, this can be an obstacle to evangelistic impact.

Cross-cultural understanding is not only important in reaching out to Chinese students and scholars but is essential in Chinese and Americans working together. This demands commitment to the relationships, determination to learn and understand important, humility. We have been helped greatly in und... cross-cultural relationships through Duane Elmer's books and teaching, particularly his book *Cross-Cultural Conflict: Building Relationships for Effective Ministry*. Dr. Elmer shares personal experiences of how our cultural backgrounds determine what we say and what we hear. When two people from different cultures think they are communicating, often they are surprised to find that much has been missed and/or misinterpreted. Another helpful book in this area is Erin Meyer's *The Culture Map*. Dr. Meyer is a professor and cross-cultural consultant for businesses worldwide. She has put together a map of cultural differences with definitions, that helps the reader to begin to realize the importance of understanding our differences in order to properly communicate and build trust. Of significant note to our discussion is her map of communication. On one end of the scale is low context communicating and the other end is high context. Dr. Meyer defines low-context as precise, simple and clear, with messages expressed and understood at face value. High-context is sophisticated, nuanced and layered with message often implied but not plainly expressed. The US culture is the most low-context of all cultures and the Chinese culture is extremely high-context. Meyer quotes Elisabeth Shen:

> When Chinese vaguely express an idea or an opinion, the real message is often just implied. They expect their conversational partner to be highly involved and to take an active role in deciphering messages, as well as in mutually creating meaning. In Chinese culture, children are taught not to just hear the explicit words but also to focus on *how* something is said, and on what is *not* said. (p.48)

Therefore, when an American team member thinks that they have made things clear, what is understood and the response that they receive often does not mean what they think. And when a Chinese team member caringly shares their perspectives by implying a message within the verbal communication, they are often surprised when their American colleagues do not get it. The only remedy to this difficulty is to work diligently together by asking questions with humility to make sure there is understanding.

Chapter 17

The Importance of Unity and Harmony

Jesus prays in John 17 "that all of them may be one, Father, just as you are in me and I am in you. May they also be in us so that the world may believe that you have sent me." The purpose of unity and oneness among Christians is that the world will believe in Jesus.

In our research, some of those interviewed indicated that they were drawn to Christ by seeing love and harmony among believers, and others said that they had some struggles in believing when they saw Christians not getting along.

Chinese coming to America are overwhelmed with the variety of religious groups, particularly the number of Christian denominations and ministries. Often the question is asked, "Why are there so many different groups, and what should I believe?" This is a challenge to answer appropriately. At COM, we share that the Bible is God's guide for us, and he tells us the way to himself through Jesus. There are a variety of Christian denominations because God has made us all different, with different cultures, personalities, interests, backgrounds, etc. God has created diversity, and so he works through many groups, but the key is to hold to the truth of the Bible and Jesus. With this answer comes the challenge of cooperating together for God's Kingdom. At COM we value cooperation for the sake of the gospel. We strive to cooperate with like-minded, committed Christians. We have found that when there is a humble heart of cooperation, there is power in communicating the gospel.

Jesus said in John 13:35, "By this everyone will know that you are my disciples, if you love one another." The impact of love is the work of God. Those outside of the faith cannot deny the attraction of a loving community in the midst of a world torn by hate and distrust. Therefore, we must work hard to love one another, to practice the "one-anothers" of the New Testament, and especially pray that God will unite us.

We would encourage anyone who is involved in university-based outreach to research and discover what is already taking place on campus and to strive to work cooperatively in reaching out to Chinese students and scholars. This may include cooperation with American and Chinese churches, other ministry organizations, volunteers, and international student office leadership. It is dangerous and unproductive to assume that we alone are called to this work and are God's special emissaries.

The business world has discovered God's truth that when we work together as a team, there is a special dynamic that is productive and powerful. Patrick Lencioni, in his book, *The Characteristics of a Team Player* gives three qualities to look for in a person: humility, hunger and smarts. *Humility* is a willingness to consider others as better than ourselves and a desire to see others succeed. *Hunger* relates to passion and calling for ministry. *Smarts* is emotional intelligence tied to experience and knowledge. It includes the ability to understand the situation, the perspectives of others and appropriate responses. If these three characteristics are evident in a team member, the success of the team and ministry will be accelerated. If there is a missing link or weakness in any of these areas, there will be difficulty in working together as a team and ministry effectiveness will be limited.

Gerry, Sam and Kristen are all committed Christians, have followed God's leading in their lives and have committed themselves to campus ministry among Chinese. They serve together as part of a staff team on a campus where the opportunities to reach out to Chinese are great and increasing. There is a good network of Christians involved. But there have been limits to the ministry due to the struggles of working together. There have been differences in personality and style of ministry. The solution has been for each one to "do their own thing." There has been tension not only among themselves, but with volunteers and cooperating churches because of the division among staff. Things are beginning to improve, however, as Lencioni's three ingredients have become an increasing part of their lives, individually and in community. The team leader has begun to take more responsibility to lead and care for the others. The team members have begun to submit themselves to the leader and desire to work together. Humility is rising — an interesting phrase, since humility involves the lowering of one's self. The hunger for ministry was always there, but working together has increased effectiveness, even while ministry is difficult. The result has been an increase in smarts. Individually, the team members are learning what it takes to succeed. As they submit to each other and work from their shared passion, they are learning to understand each other and to appreciate their differences. These differences are becoming strengths instead of weaknesses that divide. Others are noticing, and are attracted to the team. A new staff member joined and understands the struggles of the team in the past, has great hope and excitement about the future.

The cooperation of multiple ministries is also very powerful. Several university locations in key cities of North America have seen a successful partnership of international student ministries. These groups consist of individuals, churches and mission organizations reaching out to Chinese students and scholars, who are working together to accomplish more and to demonstrate that Christians love one another. Some examples of cities where strategic partnerships have formed are: Portland, Oregon; Philadelphia, Pennsylvania; Boston, Massachusetts; Saint Louis, Missouri; Los Angeles, California; Manhattan, Kansas; and Virginia Beach, Virginia. All of these groups have connections with ACMI, the Association of Christians Ministering Among Internationals, which is a networking organization to encourage partnerships for the growth of the ministry to international students.

Part Four

Looking to the Future

Chapter 18

Will China Rise as a Christian Nation?

Before we address this question, it is helpful to look at both China today and the bigger picture of China in its historical context. Powerful social and cultural forces have been at work in China. The Chinese people have become disillusioned about the communist ideology. The government has lost its moral credibility in the eyes of the people. What is holding China together seems to be the government's ability to generate economic growth and create wealth for its people. But the economy cannot be always growing. China's growing market economy has given people wealth and personal freedoms, but not meaning, hope or purpose in life. In the whirlwind of China's rapid changes, contradictions and uncertainties, social fabrics are breaking down; the old community and safety nets have gone. Chinese people are struggling to know what is going on around them; they are craving for a sense of community, something spiritual that could help anchor their lives and provide needed perspectives.

Globalization is impacting China in a profound way. Due to the flow of information and the powerful witness of faithful Christians,

Christianity is being seen in an increasingly positive light. More Chinese people are becoming aware of the outside world and are being exposed to Christian beliefs and practices. Contrary to government propaganda, the Chinese are now seeing that they can be Christian, educated, and respected—while living a normal life with dignity and decency. Despite the tension between the Chinese and Western governments, many Chinese people admire how people live in countries where Christian influence has been strong. Many Chinese—especially its intellectuals—attribute the success stories of the West to the influence of Christian belief and values.

Despite many positive developments, it is still too early to predict if China will rise as a Christian nation. However, we think it is appropriate to humbly keep our minds open to future possibilities.

What exactly is a Christian nation?

We need to address this question before going further. The term "Christian nation" is controversial, and people may have different definitions along with an array of connotations. For our purposes, and due to lack of better terms, we are defining a Christian nation as having a significant number of Christians among its population.

By this definition, many countries today are already Christian nations. Christians have already made a significant positive contribution in these nations. Of course, that does not mean these countries are perfect or without their own challenges; nor does it mean that their elected leaders make decisions in light of Christian values. These countries remain as secular states, as they should be. Secular as they are, they are tempered and often influenced by the values of their Christian citizens. We believe that a growing Christian population makes a difference in a nation. Once the Christian population reaches a critical mass, Christian values—such as love, mercy, justice, peace, good will, stewardship, respect for human dignity, authority and rule of law—will gradually become more admired and accepted in society, regardless of the political system of the country. Such values may be accepted without being labeled as Christian. If that is the case, then China is on its way to becoming such a nation.

The mere presence of Christians is often a blessing to society. This happens when Christians seek to live out Christlike character and values individually and corporately, and through their professions as businessmen, teachers, engineers, accountants, writers, artists, lawyers and government officials. As many small streams join to form a roaring river, so is the transforming influence of such Christians as they contribute to nation building and become agents of God's blessing. Even before the communist takeover of China in 1949, many Chinese Christians returned after completing their studies in Western countries and became agents of transformation. The lives and contributions of such Chinese believers are well documented in *Salt and Light,* a book series by Carol Lee Hamrin and Stacey Bieler. The difference is that the number of Chinese studying in the West and returning to China is now far greater, and the potential contribution to China's nation building greatly exceeds that of the past.

It may sound ironic that China could become a Christian nation. There are several obvious reasons for this. Culturally, Buddhism has had a long history in China, having been deeply rooted for over two thousand years among the majority Han Chinese people. Politically, the Chinese government has strongly advocated atheism as its official dogma and has enforced atheist thinking through the school system. In China, all religions and belief systems have been suppressed in one way or another. However, in the past few decades, statistics have confirmed a strong growth of Christianity in China. If the growth trend continues — and that is a big if — then China may become one of the countries with the largest Christian populations.

Christianity's rapid growth has caught the attention of many China observers and research institutes. On April 19, 2014 *The Telegraph* published a story on the growth of Christianity in China. The article says:

> "The number of Christians in Communist China is growing so steadily that by 2030 it could have more churchgoers than America...
>
> Officially, the People's Republic of China is an atheistic country but that is changing fast as many of its 1.3 billion citizens seek meaning and spiritual comfort that neither communism nor capitalism seem to have supplied.
>
> Christian congregations in particular have skyrocketed since churches began reopening when Chairman Mao's death in 1976 signaled the end of the Cultural Revolution.
>
> Less than four decades later, some believe China is now poised to become not just the world's number one economy but also its most numerous Christian nation....
>
> China's Protestant community, which had just one million members in 1949, has already overtaken those of countries more commonly associated with an evangelical boom. In 2010 there were more than 58 million Protestants in China compared to 40 million in Brazil and 36 million in South Africa, according to the Pew Research Centre's Forum on Religion and Public Life.

Prof Yang, a leading expert on religion in China, believes that number will swell to around 160 million by 2025. That would likely put China ahead even of the United States, which had around 159 million Protestants in 2010 but whose congregations are in decline.

By 2030, China's total Christian population, including Catholics, would exceed 247 million, placing it above Mexico, Brazil and the United States as the largest Christian congregation in the world, he predicted.

"Mao thought he could eliminate religion. He thought he had accomplished this," Prof Yang said. "It's ironic — they didn't. They actually failed completely."

According to Dr. David Aikman, former Time magazine Beijing bureau chief and author of *Jesus in Beijing,* China as a nation has a Christian future:

"China is in the process of becoming Christianized. That does not mean that all Chinese will become Christian, or even that a majority will. But at the present rate of growth…, it is possible that Christians will constitute 20 to 30 percent of China's population within three decades. If that should happen, it is almost certain that a Christian view of the world will be the dominant worldview within China's political and cultural establishment, and possibly also within senior military circles."

It seems that some of China's top leaders must have thought of the benefits of adopting Christian values or even making Christianity the official religion of China. In *Jesus in Beijing,* Aikman describes a private event when China's President Jiang Zemin attended a private dinner party in the home of another senior political leader in Beijing in 2002:

> The conversation turned to the Party's upcoming Sixteenth Congress, a momentous, once-every-five years gathering then scheduled for the late autumn of 2002 (the Congress convened November 7-15, 2002).

> The company was relaxed, the mood ebullient. "Comrade Jiang," a guest asked, "if, before leaving office, you could make one decree that you knew would be obeyed in China, what would it be?" Jiang put on a broad smile and looked around the room. "I would make Christianity the official religion of China," he replied.

Obviously, Jiang was not being serious about going forward with this idea by using the power of his position just before leaving office. As Aikman keenly observed, however, "even if he were being merely playful with his fellow guests, his whimsical comment was telling."

China's leaders know that Chinese people no longer believe in communism as a belief system; nor do they believe in the Chinese government as a political institution. The leaders also know that China is facing alarming moral decline and lack of basic ethics. There is widespread irresponsibility in almost all sectors of society, and high levels of greed and corruption. The government seems to be able to manage China's economic growth, but at a loss in knowing how to deal with the soft issues of society—matters of the heart. The leaders know these problems are not within their power to solve. It is not far-fetched that the top leadership must have looked at Christianity and asked what it could offer to China. But if the Chinese government does become open to Christian values and even adopt them, it will not likely be because the leaders themselves are truly converted in the religious sense. Rather, they may embrace these values for practical reasons, hoping that Christianity will be good for China and helpful in dealing with its problems.

From a theological viewpoint, Christians should not be surprised by the possibility of China becoming a Christian nation. Throughout the Bible, we see our God playing an active role in human history and behind the rise and fall of empires. History is, after all, *His* story. Despite the many tragedies in human history, we Christians are a hopeful people—not only because God ultimately triumphs at the end, but because God is at work throughout the span of human history.

Miraculous shifts occur in history because God's hand is behind them. One such historical example is the Roman Empire openly embracing Christianity during the reign of Constantine. It is an academic exercise to debate whether he embraced Christianity due to his own religious beliefs, or, as a wise politician, he endorsed it because of the undeniable growth trend of Christianity in the empire. What is important is that the Roman Empire that had once persecuted Christianity turned around and embraced it.

What had previously seemed to be impossible for the Roman Empire became a reality. As we look back at that period of time, we tend to see it academically or as just a fact of history, without appreciating the utter surprise people must have felt. We believe a similar surprise may be coming for China, God willing.

An article in the May/June 2015 edition of *Foreign Affairs* included a graph showing that the number of Christians in China is growing significantly faster than the number of Chinese in the Communist Party (see next page). Very few communist party members truly believe in communism in their hearts. They become members for the sake of convenience because Party membership helps them in their career path and with job promotions. In contrast, Chinese become Christians because they believe in God and want to following teachings in the Bible. Most Chinese believers are first generation believers; they choose their Christian faith rather than inherit if from their parents. The result is a far greater commitment, as well as shared common values among Christians.

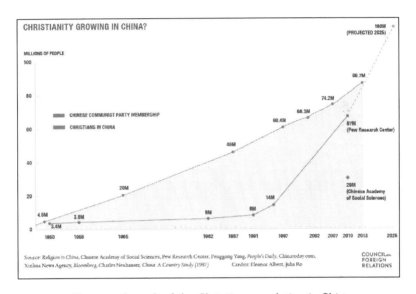

Figure 3. Growth of the Christian population in China

Thus, China is now on the track toward an uncharted future. It would be surprising to many, but not unforeseeable, if China emerges not only as an economic world power but also as a Christian nation, defined as Christians comprising a significant percentage of the population, making a significant contribution to the society and culture. China is already heading in that direction in terms of the numerical growth of the Christian church.

According to a Pew Research article, "Religion in China on the Eve of the 2008 Beijing Olympics", written on May 2, 2008:

Christianity is China's second-largest officially recognized religion. The Horizon surveys indicate that less than 4% of the adult population identifies as Christian, but there is indirect evidence that suggests this number could be low...

Chinese government figures indicate dramatic growth among Protestants and Catholics, as is seen by comparing the numbers reported in the government's 1997 White Paper on religion with an updated 2006 "Background Brief" provided to the Pew Forum by the Chinese Embassy in Washington, D.C. The officially reported number of Christians increased from 14 million to 21 million, or 50%, in less than 10 years. During this time, Protestants increased from 10 million to 16 million — a 60% increase — and Catholics from 4 million to 5 million — a 25% increase. While some of this growth may be due to independent Christians registering with the official Protestant and Catholic associations, the new background brief goes so far as to say that Protestantism, in particular, has increased "by more than 20 times" since it "was first brought to China in the early 19th century."

The Pew Research article also points out that there the total number of Christians is likely greater that the official number provided by the Chinese government:

The Holy Spirit Study Centre in Hong Kong, which monitors Catholics worshipping in congregations that do not affiliate with the state-approved Catholic association, estimates that there are at least 12 million Catholics in China, 7 million more than acknowledged by the government.[1] There is some indirect survey

---

1   http://www.hsstudyc.org.hk/en/china/en_cinfo_china_stat06.html

evidence that suggests the existence of a potentially large number of unaffiliated, independent Christians. For example, the 2005 Pew survey found that 6% of the Chinese public expresses belief in the possible existence of "God/Jesus" (in Chinese *Shangdi/Yesu*), a rough equivalent of saying the "Christian God." This is more than 50% higher than the number of people who self-identify as a Christian in the same poll. The 6% estimate is closer to the estimates of China's total Christian population made by religious demographers and researchers.

While the exact number may be impossible to verify, it seems clear that all sources of information are painting the same picture of a fast growing church in China.

Chapter 19

Concerns about China and Our Response — How Do We Make a Difference?

The *Wall Street Journal* carried an article titled "China Flexes Economic Muscle Throughout Burgeoning Africa." China has been expanding its influence in war-torn nations in Africa by supplying economic aid. The result will be a relationship that leads to economic interdependence in the future and the strengthening of China as a world power. These moves of influence by China send waves of concern throughout the US government — concerns related to threats to the nation's security, and loss of resources from other nations who have now turned to China to help meet their needs. These are appropriate concerns, but what is the best solution?

Hebrews 12:14 says, "Make every effort to live in peace with all men and to be holy." There is no doubt in my mind that the best solution is found in developing trusting, friendship relationships that go beyond economic and political boundaries. And one of the key areas where this is happening is with the Chinese scholars studying at American universities. God has opened the door in new ways to connect with people of influence. These opportunities for friendships are with medical researchers, city managers, engineers, professors, and even government officials — many people who will influence decisions for the future of China. In another *Wall Street Journal* article, "China's Study-Abroad Program," the author states, "The Chinese government has made it a priority to promote people who have had some education abroad. Senior officials in China's finance, foreign-affairs, science-and-technology and education ministries hold degrees from foreign universities or have been visiting scholars abroad...in some agencies the figure is as high as 75%."

Recently, a campus staff team shared concern on how to make contact with the Chinese scholars, since the university would not give out contact information. Our staff responded to a bulletin board note from a Chinese scholar requesting help in English. As they met weekly, a caring relationship developed. The Chinese scholar was a person of influence and position in China, and was in charge of approving people to attend this university program. He told our campus staff that he wanted all that came to the university from China to meet him and he would send the names and information of those who are coming and encourage them to meet our staff. God leads, provides and opens doors!

Chapter 20

The Critical Role of China's Intellectuals

If China is ever to emerge as a Christian nation, it is critical that China's intellectuals respond positively to the Christian message.

A transformation has been taking place in China beyond what the media headlines can capture. Powerful forces, both spiritual and secular, are at work. The Chinese people once naively believed in communism but have long become disillusioned about it since the death of China's Chairman Mao in 1976. The Chinese government has de facto abandoned communist ideology and instead openly embraced a capitalist market economy. But, despite its ideological bankruptcy, for the sake of face-saving, the Chinese government has kept the name of communist for its political party and has insisted that its economy is a "socialist" free market. However, neither communism nor capitalism has been able to offer meaning or purpose to the Chinese people. Many people in China have become dismayed and confused by the shifts in ideology and moral standards, and they are searching for answers for themselves, their families, and their country.

Among the people searching for answers are China's intellectuals.

The term "intellectuals" in China's context normally refers to the cultural elites at its core and can generally be extended to include all of the thinking, educated people in China who have university degrees. They see themselves at the forefront of China's destiny, responsible for China's future wellbeing—and they take their roles seriously. If China is ever to become Christian in any significant way, the view of China's intellectuals toward Christianity will make a critical difference.

Closing Thoughts

We hope that what you have read will inspire you to either get involved with reaching out to Chinese students and scholars while they are in the United States, or to continue and deepen your ministry if you are already involved. We would love to hear from you and partner with you in this very important opportunity! You can reach us at China Outreach Ministries by visiting chinaoutreach.org.

About the Authors

Dr. Glen Osborn served as President of China Outreach Ministries from 2002-2017 and continues to serve as Minister at Large. Glen and wife Betty have three married children and seven grandchildren. He has degrees from Rowan University, Wheaton Graduate School, and Columbia International University. He enjoys playing the trumpet, golf, and riding with Betty on their Honda Goldwing.

Rev. Daniel B. Su (蘇百達) is the President of China Outreach Ministries. He has served with COM in various capacities since 1991 following his graduation from Liberty Baptist Theological Seminary in Lynchburg, Virginia. He experienced God's amazing blessings in church planting and pastoring in the Houston area from 2006 to 2013. Daniel came to know Christ as a teenager in China's House Church Movement before coming to America for college in 1986. God has gifted him with bi-lingual and bi-cultural background. He lives in Pennsylvania with his wife Beth and two children.

References Cited

Aikman, David. 2006. *Jesus in Beijing: How Christianity is Transforming China and Changing the Global Balance of Power.* Washington, DC: Regnery Faith.

Allison, Graham and Robert Blackwell. 2013. Interview: Lee Kuan Yew on the future of U.S.—China relations. *The Atlantic*, March 5.

Bays, Daniel. 2011. *A New History of Christianity in China.* Hoboken, NJ: Wiley-Blackwell.

Bieler, S. 2004. *"Patriots" or "Traitors": A history of American-educated Chinese students.* Armonk, NY: M.E. Sharpe.

Daban, M.R. 2004. *Chinese Christians in North America.* Tripod.

Elmer, Duane. 1994. *Cross-Cultural Conflict: Building Relationships for Effective Ministry.* Downers Grove, IL: IVP Academic.

Garrod, Andrew and Jay Davis, editors. 1999. *Crossing customs: International students write on U.S. college life and culture.* New York, NY: Falmer Press.

Guiness, Os. 1996. *God in the dark: The assurance of faith beyond a shadow of a doubt.* Wheaton, IL: Crossway Books.

Hamrin, Lee Carol, 2009. *Salt and Light, Volume 1: Lives of Faith That Shaped Modern China.* Eugene, OR: Wipf and Stock Publishers.

Houssney, Georges. 2013. Factors leading to conversion of Muslims to Christ. *Biblical Missiology*, April 8, 2013. http://biblicalmissiology. org/2013/ 04/08/factors-leading-to-conversion-of-muslims-to-christ/

Kraft, Charles H. 1979 *Christianity in Culture.* Maryknoll, NY: Orbis.

_____1992. "Allegiance, Truth and Power Encounters in Christian Witness." In Pentecost, Mission and Ecumenism: Essays On Intercultural Theology. Jan A.B. Jongeneel. ed. Frankfurt: Peter Lang.

Lau, Lawson. 1984. *The world at your doorstep: a handbook for international student ministry.* Downers Grove, IL: InterVarsity Press.

Lencioni, Patrick. 2016. *The Ideal Team Player: How to Recognize and Cultivate the Three Essential Ingredients.* San Francisco, CA: Jossey-Bass.

Lewis, C.S. 1952. *Mere Christianity.* London, England: Macmillan.

Ling, Samuel and Stacey Bieler, editors. 1999. *Chinese intellectuals and the gospel.* San Gabriel, CA: China Horizon.

Mason, Mike. 2006. *Champagne for the Soul: Rediscovering God's Gift of Joy.* Vancouver, BC: Regent College Publishing.

Meyer, Erin. 2014. *The Culture Map: Breaking Through the Invisible Boundaries of Global Business.* New York, NY: Public Affairs.

McKnight, Scot. 2002. *Turning to Jesus: The sociology of conversion in the Gospels.* Louisville, KY: Westminster John Knox Press.

McMurrie, Beth. 2012. China continues to drive foreign-student growth in the United States. *The Chronicle of Higher Education.* November 12, 2012. http://chronicle.com/article/China-Continues-to-Drive/135700 (accessed September 4, 2014).

Newman, Jonah. 2014. Almost one-third of all foreign students in U.S. are from China. The Chronicle of Higher Education. February 7, 2014. http://chronicle.com/blogs/data/2014/02/07/almost-one-third-of-all-foreign-students-are-from-china/ (accessed September 5, 2014).

Osburn, Robert. 2005. Religious experiences of Buddhist, Muslim, and Christian international students: A case at the University of Minnesota. Ph.D. diss., University of Minnesota.

Peace, Richard V. 1999. *Conversion in the New Testament: Paul and the twelve.* Grand Rapids, MI: William B. Eerdmans Publishing Co.

Rambo, Lewis. 1993. *Understanding religious conversion.* New Haven, CT: Yale University Press.

Rawson, Katie. 1999. Evangelizing East Asian students in the United States with special reference to media tools. DMin diss., Fuller Theological Seminary.

Roembke, Lianne. 2000. *Building credible multicultural teams.* Pasadena, CA: William Carey Library.

Su, Edwin. 1991. *Mainland Chinese in America: An emerging kinship.* Paradise, PA: Ambassadors for Christ, Inc.

Wang, Yuting and Fenggang Yang. 2006. More than evangelical and ethnic: the ecological factor in Chinese conversion to Christianity in the United States. *Sociology of Religion.* 67:2

Wong, Lai Fan. 2006. From atheists to evangelicals: The Christian conversion experience of mainland Chinese intellectuals in the U.S.A. ThD Diss., Boston University School of Theology.

Wu, Jackson. 2013. *Saving God's face: A Chinese contextualization of salvation through honor and shame.* Pasadena, CA: WCIU Press.

Yang, Fenggang. 1998. Chinese conversion to evangelical Christianity: The importance of Social and Cultural Contexts. *Sociology of Religion,* 59:3

————1999. *Chinese Christians in America: Conversion, assimilation, and adhesive identities.* University Park, PA: Pennsylvania State University Press.

_____2005. Lost in the market, saved at McDonald's: Conversion to Christianity in urban China. *Journal for the Scientific Study of Religion,* 44(4), 423-441.

Yew, Lee Kuan. 2013. *Lee Kuan Yew: The grand master's insights on China, the United States, and the world.* Cambridge, MA: The MIT Press.

友愛中华 China Outreach
MINISTRIES
Giving Christ to China's Future Leaders

China Outreach Ministries shares Christ's love with
Chinese students and scholars on North American
campuses, serving them, reaching them with the Good
News, discipling them, and helping them become godly
leaders for Christ who share their faith with others.

We serve these men and women by:

*Building Christ-like relationships with
Chinese students and scholars.*

*Offering programs and practical services that
demonstrate Christian love and concern.*

*Leading investigative Bible studies
and other outreach activities.*

*Providing discipleship training
for those who become believers.*

*Equipping believers to return to
China as effective witnesses for Christ.*

*Enlisting and training skilled Chinese and non-Chinese
staff who are called by the Lord to serve in Christian
ministry among the Chinese.*

Contact us at:
China Outreach Ministries

555 Gettysburg Pike, Suite A-200
Mechanicsburg, PA 17055

Phone: 717-591-3500 | Fax: 717-591-0412
1-800-269-7815 | chinaoutreach.org

COM is a member of the Evangelical Council for Financial Accountability.

Made in the USA
Columbia, SC
02 November 2017